I S L A M

A Challenge to the Christian Church

Stanford E. Murrell

I c h t h u s *Publications* • Apollo, Pennsylvania

Our goal is to provide high-quality, thought-provoking books that foster encouragement and spiritual growth. For more information regarding Ichthus Publications, other IP books, or bulk purchases, visit us online or write to support@ichthuspublications.com.

Unless otherwise indicated, all Scripture quotations are taken from the New King James Version®. Copyright © 1982 by Thomas Nelson. Used by permission. All rights reserved.

Printed in the United States of America

Islam: A Challenge to the Christian Church

ISBN: 978-1-946971-08-1

ICHTHUS

www.ichthuspublications.com

"Choose for yourselves this day whom you will serve."

—Joshua 24:15

Contents

Introduction

A Religion in Corruption?

"Ignorance is bliss"—at least that's what eighteenth-century English poet Thomas Gray told us in his famous poem.[1] There, he nostalgically recalled the carefree days of his youth, unmarred by the poignant and dark realities inherent in adulthood. What Gray inferred by his axiomatic statement is that not only is ignorance bliss but, conversely, knowledge is despair (or at least the awareness of it is).

There is all too frequently—lest we succumb to despair—a reluctance to express or to acknowledge publicly what is known to be true in order to make us feel better, or simply because it is oftentimes easier to ignore than to confront. What we should know, or could know, but don't know, or refuse to know, permits us to feel better. Nowhere is this "ignorance-is-bliss" attitude more evident—in the Western world, at least—than in the realm of religion, specifically, the religion of Islam. Consider a few examples. Less than one week after the 9/11 terrorist attacks in New York City, former President George W. Bush reassured a reeling nation that, "These acts of violence against innocents

---

[1] *Ode on a Distant Prospect of Eton College.*

violate the fundamental tenets of the Islamic faith . . . Islam is peace."[2] President Bush elsewhere continued to insist that, "Islam, as practiced by the vast majority of people, is a peaceful religion, a religion that respects others."[3] America's ensuing leader similarly expressed this same sentiment regarding Islam. Then President Barack Obama made this announcement at a speech to the Islamic Society of Baltimore in February 2016: "So let's start with this fact: For more than a thousand years, people have been drawn to Islam's message of peace. And the very word itself, Islam, comes from *salam*—peace."[4]

The examples of leaders pronouncing, "Islam is a religion of peace," are ubiquitous and endless, but the message seems to be at odds with other evidence. Al Qaeda, the Islamic State of Iraq and Syria (ISIS), Boko Haram, Hezbollah, Hamas, and other radical terrorist groups kill in the name of Allah and the prophet Muhammad; homosexuals are stoned to death in countries that practice Sharia Law; women can be—and have been—stoned to death for being raped; teenage girls are often forced to undergo cliterectomies;[5] women are, by Islamic law, subservient and possess fewer rights than males (just travel to any Muslim country for

---

[2] See https://georgewbush-whitehouse.archives.gov/news/releases/ 2001/09/200 10917-11.html (accessed July 8, 2017).

[3] Remarks by President George W. Bush in a statement to reporters during a meeting with U.N. Secretary General Kofi Annan at the Oval Office, Washington, D.C. November 13, 2002. https://georgewbush-whitehouse.archives.gov/infocus/ ramadan/islam.html (accessed July 8, 2017).

[4] https://obamawhitehouse.archives.gov/the-press-office/2016/02/03/remarks-pr esident-islamic-society-baltimore (accessed July 8, 2017).

[5] See a tragic example of one woman's defense of the practice as a guest on Tucker Carlson: http://www.thegatewaypundit.com/2017/05/horror-woman-defen ds-female-genital-mutilation-young-girls-video/ (accessed July 8, 2017).

empirical proof of this statement); honor killings for those who bring shame on a family number in the thousands worldwide annually. The examples are myriad and yet the response is seemingly one of silence, especially from our leaders in Western countries. The silence is deafening.

Former Central Intelligence Agency (CIA) covert officer Bryan Dean Wright argues that the Western world has been intentionally delusional regarding the full truth of Islam: "Politicians should stop referring to Islam as an 'agent of peace' and say it is 'a religion in crisis.'"[6]

So which narrative is correct? Is Islam a harbinger of truth and peace as world leaders and Muslim apologists insist, or is Islam a "religion in crisis"? To answer this question correctly, we would do well to listen to the teachings of Jesus who rightly pointed out that "by their fruits you will know them" (Matt. 7:20). In other words, fruit is the telltale sign of something real, because fruit doesn't lie. Instead, fruit (or the kind of it) exposes the tree. "For a good tree does not bear bad fruit, nor does a bad tree bear good fruit. For every tree is known by its own fruit. For *men* do not gather figs from thorns, nor do they gather grapes from a bramble bush" (Luke 6:43–44).

So that inevitably leads us to ask: Who gets to decide which version of Islam better portrays the teachings of Islam? The Muslim neighbor in the suburbs of Southeast Florida will inevitably look different than the Imam preaching in Saudi Arabia. One way to resolve this seeming tension is to harken back to the

---

[6] See https://www.yahoo.com/news/former-cia-officer-stop-calling-001733051.html (accessed July 8, 2017).

words of Jesus and the underlying figure of the fruit. What sort of fruit has Islam yielded? Better yet, what fruit did its founder, Muhammad, yield? How was Islam expressed through the words, deeds, and practices of this sixth-century man from the Arabian city of Mecca? The *Qur'an* confidently proclaims in the moral supremacy of Muhammad, and exalts him as a man whom everyone is to emulate. "There has certainly been for you in the Messenger of Allah an excellent pattern for anyone whose hope is in Allah and the Last Day and [who] remembers Allah often" (Surah 33:21). And yet how does he compare to the life, practice, and teachings of Jesus?

For starters, there is abundant historical evidence that Islam is not a religion of peace and was never intended to be as such. Consider the life of Muhammad and the chaos that ensued. Under his leadership and approval—to cite just one example—up to 900 citizens of Banu Qurayza, a Jewish tribe, were beheaded in A.D. 627. The event is referenced in the *Qur'an*.

> "And He brought down those who supported them among the People of the Scripture from their fortresses and cast terror into their hearts [so that] a party you killed, and you took captive a party. And He caused you to inherit their land and their homes and their properties and a land which you have not trodden. And ever is Allah, over all things, competent" (Surah 33:26–27).[7]

---

[7] The English translation of the *Qur'an* has been taken from Sahih International.

The history of the spread of Islam is the story of violence, with a view to conquer anyone, and everyone, that had resources to be enjoyed by confiscation and theft. The adherents of Islam are conditioned by history, by culture, by the *Qur'an*, and by example, to be aggressive towards others. Women in particular do not fare well, because women, under Islamic law, are viewed as property to be owned by men.

> "Men are in charge of women by [right of] what Allah has given one over the other and what they spend [for maintenance] from their wealth. So righteous women are devoutly obedient, guarding in [the husband's] absence what Allah would have them guard. But those [wives] from whom you fear arrogance—[first] advise them; [then if they persist], forsake them in bed; and [finally], strike them. But if they obey you [once more], seek no means against them. Indeed, Allah is ever Exalted and Grand" (Surah 4:34).

America's experience with the Islamic religion has been anything but peaceful from her infancy and warring with the Barbary pirates during the presidency of Thomas Jefferson down to the current global war on terrorism since the Islamic terrorist attacks on 9/11. It was faithful practitioners of the Islamic religion who knowingly, willfully, and deliberately hijacked planes for the sole purpose to "kill the polytheists wherever you find them and capture them and besiege them and sit in wait for them at every place of ambush." (Surah 9:5) And, in so doing, in killing infidels and dying for the cause of Allah, those hijackers thought they were to be ushered into Paradise to enjoy unending sensual gratification with "fair women with large [beautiful] eyes." (Surah 52:20)

Jesus taught us to examine, not only individuals by their fruits, but religious systems as well. The fruit of Islam, when viewed worldwide and in its totality, is striking. This small book on Islam is not simply to communicate anti-Islamic sentiments or just to "preach to the choir." Instead, it is designed to offer hope to those who share in the belief of one God, the God of Abraham, Isaac, and Jacob. It is designed to provoke self-reflection for those practitioners of an ancient religion to look afresh at what their religion has wrought to the world. It is a plea, in part, to Muslims who desire to have a personal relationship with the Creator, with a God who entered His own creation, because He so loved the world that He sent His Son to die for the sins of those who would believe in Him (John 3:16).

Jesus told us that we would know something by its fruit. It is long past time to reexamine the fruit set before us in the religion of Islam. Listen, then, with ears anew and an open mind and discover the true fruit can only be found in the person and work of Jesus— and in no other.

No matter how dogmatic our leaders might sound about the religion of Islam, no matter how earnestly they tell us we all worship the same God but in various expression—the truth uttered by Jesus remains the same: "I am the way, the truth, and the life. No one comes to the Father except through Me" (John 14:6).

Adam Murrell
Apollo, Pennsylvania

"The ambassador answered us that [the right] was founded on the Laws of the Prophet, that it was written in their Koran, that all nations who should not have answered their authority were sinners, that it was their right and duty to make war upon them wherever they could be found, and to make slaves of all they could take as prisoners, and that every Mussulman who should be slain in battle was sure to go to Paradise."

—Thomas Jefferson[1]

---

[1] Jefferson explains in a letter to Secretary of State John Jay the answer provided to him by Ambassador Sidi Haji Abdrahaman in reply to the question by what right Muslim Barbary pirates extorted money and took slaves.

ONE

A Brief Overview of Islam

I slam, the third of the major monotheistic religions, can be traced to a sixth-century man named Muhammad who lived in the Arabian Peninsula. Muhammad was born into a family belonging to a clan of Quraish, a ruling tribe of Mecca in A.D. 570. Muhammad's father died before he was born, and his mother passed away leaving him an orphan when he was six years old. From there he was consigned to the care of his grandfather, the head of a clan, but he too died, and Muhammad was then cared for by his uncle.

Not much is known about the boy's adolescence. However, Muslim tradition tells us he was known as *al-ameen*, "the trustworthy," so he may have had a reputation for honesty in his trading and dealings as a tradesman. Around the year A.D. 590, Muhammad entered the service of a merchant widow named Khadijah, some fifteen years his senior. Sometime later she asked him to marry her, and he accepted her proposal. They had two sons together, both of whom died, and four daughters.

At the age of 40, in the year A.D. 610, he retreated to a cave on Mount Hira to meditate and began having a series of visions. He also heard a voice, later attributed to the angel Gabriel, which ordered him to: "Recite in the name of your Lord who created— Created man from a clinging substance" (Surah 96:1–2). Muhammad's visions continued over the ensuing 22 years until his death in A.D. 632. Although Muhammad claimed knowledge and revelations from the one true God, he and those who followed his teachings claimed to be neither Jews nor Christians, but descendants of Abraham, through Ishmael.

The Story of Ishmael

Ishmael was the son of the Hebrew patriarch Abraham, but not the one according to divine promise. Instead, he became the eldest son of Abraham by Hagar, his Egyptian concubine. "So Hagar bore Abram a son; and Abram named his son, whom Hagar bore, Ishmael. Abram *was* eighty-six years old when Hagar bore Ishmael to Abram" (Gen. 16:15–16). Ishmael was born when Abraham was eighty-six years old, fourteen years before the birth of Isaac (Gen. 21:5), around 2076 B.C. in Mamre.

As the son of Abraham, through the Egyptian slave Hagar, Ishmael was loved and prayed for. "And Abraham said to God, "Oh, that Ishmael might live before You!" (Gen. 17:18).

The Lord's answer to this request, however was, "No." Ishmael would not be the fulfillment of the covenant promise. But he would be blessed and become the father of a great nation.

> "Then God said: 'No, Sarah your wife shall bear you a
> son, and you shall call his name Isaac; I will establish My
> covenant with him for an everlasting covenant, *and* with

his descendants after him. ²⁰ And as for Ishmael, I have heard you. Behold, I have blessed him, and will make him fruitful, and will multiply him exceedingly. He shall beget twelve princes, and I will make him a great nation. ²¹ But My covenant I will establish with Isaac, whom Sarah shall bear to you at this set time next year' " (Gen. 17:19–21).

With this promise in his heart, Abraham took Ishmael and gave him the physical sign of being part of a covenant blessing—circumcision. At thirteen years of age, Ishmael received this outward sign of salvation—circumcision of the flesh—but his circumcision never extended to the heart; it never reached to the essence of who he was, to his soul—most importantly, to his attitude and relationship with the one true God.

> "So Abraham took Ishmael his son, all who were born in his house and all who were bought with his money, every male among the men of Abraham's house, and circumcised the flesh of their foreskins that very same day, as God had said to him. ²⁴ Abraham *was* ninety-nine years old when he was circumcised in the flesh of his foreskin. ²⁵ And Ishmael his son *was* thirteen years old when he was circumcised in the flesh of his foreskin. ²⁶ That very same day Abraham was circumcised, and his son Ishmael" (Gen. 17:23–26).

The time came when Ishmael revealed the hostility he would always have towards the true child of the covenant, Isaac. This happened when he was about fifteen or sixteen years of age. "And Sarah saw the son of Hagar the Egyptian, whom she had borne to Abraham, scoffing" (Gen. 21:9).

Because of his hostility toward Isaac, Sarah insisted that Hagar and her child be sent away. Though Abraham was reluctant to send Hagar and Ishmael away, the Lord intervened to agree with Sarah. The story is recorded in Genesis 21.

> "Therefore she said to Abraham, 'Cast out this bondwoman and her son; for the son of this bondwoman shall not be heir with my son, *namely* with Isaac.' [11] And the matter was very displeasing in Abraham's sight because of his son.
>
> [12] But God said to Abraham, 'Do not let it be displeasing in your sight because of the lad or because of your bondwoman. Whatever Sarah has said to you, listen to her voice; for in Isaac your seed shall be called. [13] Yet I will also make a nation of the son of the bondwoman, because he *is* your seed.'
>
> [14] So Abraham rose early in the morning, and took bread and a skin of water; and putting *it* on her shoulder, he gave *it* and the boy to Hagar, and sent her away. Then she departed and wandered in the Wilderness of Beersheba. [15] And the water in the skin was used up, and she placed the boy under one of the shrubs. [16] Then she went and sat down across from *him* at a distance of about a bowshot; for she said to herself, 'Let me not see the death of the boy.' So she sat opposite *him*, and lifted her voice and wept.

¹⁷ And God heard the voice of the lad. Then the angel of God called to Hagar out of heaven, and said to her, 'What ails you, Hagar? Fear not, for God has heard the voice of the lad where he *is*. ¹⁸ Arise, lift up the lad and hold him with your hand, for I will make him a great nation.'

¹⁹ Then God opened her eyes, and she saw a well of water. And she went and filled the skin with water, and gave the lad a drink. ²⁰ So God was with the lad; and he grew and dwelt in the wilderness, and became an archer. ²¹ He dwelt in the Wilderness of Paran; and his mother took a wife for him from the land of Egypt" (Gen. 21:10–21).

Ishmael escaped death in the desert to become a rugged individual skilled in hunting while living in Paran. As well, in time, his mother found for him an Egyptian wife, thereby assuring his complete and utter spiritual abandonment of any covenant blessings associated with the Son of Promise. Again, "So God was with the lad; and he grew and dwelt in the wilderness, and became an archer. He dwelt in the Wilderness of Paran; and his mother took a wife for him from the land of Egypt." (Gen. 21:20–21).

Though there is much of the story left untold, apparently Abraham stayed in the heart of both Ishmael and Isaac, for when the great Patriarch died Ishmael united with his younger brother to find a proper burial place for their father. "Then Abraham breathed his last and died in a good old age, an old man and full *of years*, and was gathered to his people. And his sons Isaac and Ishmael buried him in the cave of Machpelah, which *is* before

Mamre, in the field of Ephron the son of Zohar the Hittite" (Gen. 25:8–9).

In fulfillment of God's word, Ishmael did become the father of a great nation, with many rulers.

> "And these *were* the names of the sons of Ishmael, by their names, according to their generations: The firstborn of Ishmael, Nebajoth; then Kedar, Adbeel, Mibsam, [14] Mishma, Dumah, Massa, [15] Hadar, Tema, Jetur, Naphish, and Kedemah. [16] These *were* the sons of Ishmael and these *were* their names, by their towns and their settlements, twelve princes according to their nations. [17] These *were* the years of the life of Ishmael: one hundred and thirty-seven years; and he breathed his last and died, and was gathered to his people" (Gen. 25:13–17).

And as a father of a great nation, Ishmael had a daughter who eventually married Esau, the estranged brother of Jacob. "Esau took his wives from the daughters of Canaan: Adah the daughter of Elon the Hittite; Aholibamah the daughter of Anah, the daughter of Zibeon the Hivite; and Basemath, Ishmael's daughter, sister of Nebajoth" (Gen. 36:2–3).

Finally, Ishmael was blessed with a long life, living for more than a hundred and thirty years. "These *were* the sons of Ishmael and these *were* their names, by their towns and their settlements, twelve princes according to their nations. These *were* the years of the life of Ishmael: one hundred and thirty-seven years; and he breathed his last and died, and was gathered to his people." (Gen. 25:16–17).

The life and legacy of Ishmael has been summed up this way:

> "Ishmael appears to have been a wild and wayward child, and doubtless the perfect freedom of desert life and interaction with those who looked upon him as heir-apparent of their great chief tended to make him impatient of restraint and overbearing in his temper. His harsh treatment by Sarah, his disappointment in not becoming the heir of Abraham, and the necessity of earning a scanty living by his sword and bow would naturally wound his proud spirit and make him what the angel had predicted: 'a wild donkey of a man; his hand will be against everyone, and everyone's hand will be against him'" (Gen. 16:12).[1]

Returning to Muhammad

After three years in keeping his incredible visions, Muhammad began to recite what he heard. The content of these recitations was based on calling the people of his day from their idolatry to the one true God. For six years (A.D. 613–619), Muhammad preached and gathered a following who were willing to listen to his message. Enough people began to listen, so many, in fact, that it caused the wealthy, polytheistic mercantile class of Mecca to become concerned at his growing popularity. Muhammad's preaching, in part, against images and turning exclusively to Allah, was harming

---

[1] *The New Unger's Bible Dictionary.*

their control of the idolatrous shrine trade and their livelihood. By A.D. 622 Muhammad felt that his life was in danger. He had to flee to Medina at the invitation of the Arab tribes there. This journey to Medina is known as the *hijrah*. This migration also officially marks the beginning of the Islamic faith, for in the year A.D. 622, Muhammad assumed political power in Medina in order to validate his prophetic position. Those who submitted to his teaching, authority, and view of Allah as the one true God were called "Muslims," meaning, "one who submits (to God)". In the ensuing decade between his rise to power in Medina and his death in A.D. 632, Muhammad gave to his followers a body of administrative, political, and religious teachings that were collected after his death and put into a book called the *Qur'an* ("the recitation").

The Beliefs of Muhammad

The main beliefs in the system of Islam may be simply noted in summary form.

- There is one God called Allah, who is unitarian in his nature. Meaning, he has no partners. There is no trinity; he has no Son. He is absolutely sovereign, and is responsible for all that happens.

- God created angels. The angels are everywhere. One sits on the right shoulder recording one's good deeds; another sits on the left shoulder recording the bad deeds. On the Day of Judgment the record books are opened, and on the basis of the record therein, an individual is either rewarded or punished. Satan was formerly an angel, but turned into a *jinn*. A *jinn* is a special order of supernatural beings, supposedly created from fire. They can possess humans.

- God appointed prophets for every age. The line starts with Adam and includes Noah, Abraham, Ishmael, Jacob, Joseph, David, Solomon, Jonah, Zechariah (the father of John), and Jesus. Muhammad is the "Seal of the Prophets."

- Holy Books. God gave every prophet a holy book. From Adam to Muhammad there 124,000 prophets, and thus the same number of holy books. Unfortunately, they have all been lost except the following: (1) The *Torah*, or Law, was given to Moses; (2) The *Zabur*, or Psalms, was given to David; (3) The *Injil*, or Gospel, was given to Jesus; (4) the *Qur'an*, or Recitation, was given to Muhammad.

- The Day of Judgment. God will judge the world on the Day of Doom. There will be a balance scale to weigh the good deeds versus the bad ones. A wonderful paradise of gardens, fruit trees, streams, rivers of wine, and black-eyed virgins will be awarded to the men who have performed many good deeds. A fiery hell waits the wicked.

- The decrees of God. A Sovereign God determines everything. He is the author of evil—in the sense that He chooses to lead individuals astray whom He will—and to guide aright whom He will. No one can withstand His decree, on any point.

The Duties of Islam

The duties, or pillars, of Islam may likewise be noted in summary form.

- The *Shahadah* (the Confession of the Creed): "There is no God, but Allah, and Muhammad is the Messenger of God." To say this in faith is to be a Muslim. To renounce this is a departure from the faith, and is punishable by death.

- *Salat* (ritual prayer). Prayers are to be made five times a day: before daybreak, noontime, mid-afternoon, sunset, before retiring for the night.

- *Zakat* (giving of alms). Giving a portion of a person's income to the poor or religious causes is mandatory. Voluntary giving (*sadaqat*) is also encouraged.

- *Sawm* (keeping the thirty day fast). This is done during the lunar month of Ramadan. It comes 11 days earlier every year. The *Qur'an* is supposed to be studied during this month reading 1/30th each night.

- *Hajj* (pilgrimage). This is commanded on all that are healthy. The pilgrim is to travel to Mecca, walk around the "House of God" (the *Kaaba*) seven times, stone the devil, say prayers at the "Station of Abraham," and drink water from the well of Zamzam, in memory of Hagar and Ishmael.

- *Jihad*, (holy war—the duty of striving in the Way of God). Some Muslims say that *jihad* is not a duty, but the *Qur'an* teaches it, Muhammad practiced it, and Muslims have practiced it historically ever since. *Note:* 20.9% of the world claims to be Muslim. That growing percentage translates to approximately 1,266,000,000 people.

Attacks on Christianity:
Assault on Christian Beliefs and Scriptures

Muslims believe that the text of the Bible, the Word of God, has been corrupted and changed and that God cannot exist as Three in One—that God could not have a Son; that God could not become a man; that Jesus could not be divine; that Jesus did not die on the cross; and that no one can die for someone else.

Muhammed Claimed to be a Prophet of God

Muhammed claimed to be equal in status to Moses and Jesus.

Muhammed claimed to be the "Seal of the Prophets," meaning that he, not Jesus, was the last of the great prophets of God.

Muhammed demands obedience to his words.

Muhammed claimed Jesus prophesied of his coming.

Muslims claim Muhammed is the fulfillment of the Old Testament prophecy.

Muslims quote the false gospel of Barnabas to support claims.

Muhammed's life is the model for all mankind.

The Claim of Muhammad for the *Qur'an*

These are God's pre-existent, eternal words.

The *Qur'an* confirms all previous scriptures.

The *Qur'an* is of equal worth to all previous Scriptures.

The *Qur'an* actually supersedes all previous Scriptures.

Because of these assaults upon the Christian faith, it is important that Christians be ready to honor Christ, and the doctrines of grace.

"But sanctify the Lord God in your hearts: and be ready always to give an answer to every man that asketh you a reason of the hope that is in you with meekness and fear: [16] Having a good conscience; that, whereas they speak evil of you, as of evildoers, they may be ashamed that falsely accuse your good conversation in Christ" (1 Pet. 3:15–16).

"And the servant of the Lord must not strive; but be gentle unto all men, apt to teach, patient, [25] In meekness instructing those that oppose themselves; if God peradventure will give them repentance to the acknowledging of the truth; [26] And that they may recover themselves out of the snare of the devil, who are taken captive by him at his will" (2 Tim. 24–26).

TWO

Is Islam in Biblical Prophecy?

In the providence of the Lord, I was once encouraged to read a primer on Islam by Gene Gurganus titled, *Islam*: *Past*, *Present*, *Future*: *What Every Loyal American Needs to Know*.

The first twenty-four pages of the book are very helpful, as the author provides a brief overview of Islam (lit. "submission"), and the mindset of a militant Muslim (lit. "one who submits"). Mr. Gurganus is familiar with the *Qur'an* (lit. "recitation"), and the Muslim people having served as a pastor and church planter in Bangladesh for seventeen years, since ninety percent of the religious population in Bangladesh is Muslim.

Unfortunately, Mr. Gurganus has placed upon himself the mantle of a modern day prophet, after rejecting other modern day prophets such as C.I. Scofield. Mr. Gurganus laments, "Sorrowfully, yet understandingly, our prophecy teachers did not see Islam in prophecy. They lived too long ago. Dr. C. I. Scofield published his Study Bible in 1909, a hundred years ago."

Think about that observation. "Our prophecy teachers did not see Islam in prophecy. They lived too long ago." But did not a true Biblical prophet see far into the future? Moses made predictions about the Messiah more than fourteen hundred years before His coming (Gen. 3:15; Deut. 18:18–19). Daniel saw four hundred and ninety years into the future (Dan. 9:24–27). The idea of a prophet—one given a divine message from God; one that can say with all authority and might, "Thus saith the LORD"—not being able to foretell the future because he lived too long ago is preposterous. What is true is that Mr. Scofield has been proven to be a discredited prophet. Unless Mr. Gurganus repents he too will go down in history as a discredited prophet, or worse.

Mr. Gunganus starts his prophetic punditry with the presuppositional idea that Islam comes within the sphere of Biblical revelation as the seventh empire of Scripture. The Bible does speak of the Egyptians, the Assyrian Empire, the Babylonian Empire, the Mede-Persia Empire, the Greek Empire, and the Roman Empire. It does not speak of the Islamic (Ottoman) Empire as Mr. Gunganus asserts. A wrong premise will lead to a wrong conclusion.

Not only has Mr. Gunganus wrongly concluded that the Bible foretold of the rise of Islam and the Ottoman Empire, but he is wrong to conclude that "Rome was not a destroyer but a builder." With just a few words Roman history is rewritten, and the Biblical prophecy of Daniel 2:40 is dismissed. Mr. Gunganus asserts that Rome was not hard as iron, cruel in character, and willing to break in pieces all that opposed it. The Jews who were slaughtered en mass by the Romans in A.D. 70 would certainly disagree with this re-assessment of history. Rome was ruthless in conquering other nations, and cruel in character, reflected in the beheading of its citizens, such as the apostle Paul, the crucifixion of innocent people, including Jesus Christ, and the apostle Peter. Rome gave to its citizens the bloody and violent gladiators of the Colosseum.

There is more. Mr. Gunganus asserts that the Muslim, Mahdi,[1] and the Biblical Antichrist have "striking similarities." Eight similarities are then listed—but all without a Scriptural reference. It is the nature of modern prophetic pundits to merely assert something, rather than appeal to Scripture in context for proper exegesis. On page 32 of his book, Mr. Gunganus abandons any hesitation, and boldly asserts, "The Mahdi is the Antichrist and at the beginning of the Tribulation is a true Muslim."

Mr. Gunganus has "one more shocker" for his readers. The other modern day prophetic teachers are all wrong. Mystery Babylon is not Rome, or New York, but Mecca!

While all this is interesting, and to a point entertaining, it is also very disturbing, for many Christians are susceptible to letting sincere and passionate Bible teachers interpret the Scriptures for them in light of contemporary events. It is wrong for Bible teachers to do that, and it is unwise for Christians to allow themselves to be swept up with novel teachings, many of which are just silly, such as, when Mr. Gunganus states that the "wine of her fornication" of Revelation 17:2, is really a reference to Middle Eastern crude oil. Now that is a novel interpretation.

Daniel was given a vision of events that would take place within a time frame of four hundred and ninety years. The prophecy God gave to Daniel was fulfilled on schedule. John was

---

[1] An eschatological figure in Islamic theology who is the prophesied redeemer of Islam who will rule for a number of years before the Day of Judgement and will rid the world of evil.

given a vision of events that were to come to pass shortly, and within his generation. "The Revelation of Jesus Christ, which God gave Him to show His servants—things which must shortly take place. And He sent and signified *it* by His angel to His servant John" (Rev. 1:1).

It is unfortunate when well-meaning individuals arise to assert that all others have been wrong, and they alone know the future. The Biblical antidote against modern day prophets is very simple.

First, be a diligent student of Scriptures. "Be diligent to present yourself approved to God, a worker who does not need to be ashamed, rightly dividing the word of truth" (2 Tim. 2:15).

Second, remember there is a difference between interpretation and application. The interpretation of Scriptures demands that attention be paid to the audience to whom a passage was intended, the time period in which it was written, and the style of language that was used. Having discerned the proper interpretation of a passage, it is not wrong to seek a spiritual and personal application, for the principles of God's Word live and abide forever.

Third, be patient. While much study can be weariness to the soul, a hasty conclusion can be damaging to the cause of Christ. God has given to His people a sure word of prophecy. That is what the believer must find and embrace. "And so we have the prophetic word confirmed, which you do well to heed as a light that shines in a dark place, until the day dawns and the morning star rises in your hearts; knowing this first, that no prophecy of Scripture is of any private interpretation" (2 Pet. 1:19–20).

THREE

The Crescent Challenges the Cross

B ecause there are between five to seven million Muslims living in America, and with that number increasing annually, it is important for Christians to understand more of Islam than what is shown on cable news or depicted in movies or on television. Islam cannot simply be reduced to a violent religion and dismissed outright. Such is an oversimplification of the religion and fails to take into account the overwhelming majority of practicing Muslims go about their daily lives in peace and want nothing of the violence and hatred as demonstrated by ISIS and other radical groups.

But there are practical reasons as well. Christians must never surrender the presupposition that Islam is a logical, coherent system of teachings. That is granting the religious writings too much. Instead, Christians would do well to recognize the reason many Muslims can point to passages in the *Qur'an* and the *Hadith*[1] and rightly claim Islam teaches "peace," is because there are passages that do in fact teach peace and condemn murder and

---

[1] A collection of traditions containing alleged sayings of the prophet Muhammad that constitute the major source of guidance and beliefs for Muslims, which are in addition to the *Qur'an*.

violence. However, conversely, religious Islamic terrorists and groups such as ISIS can continue their wave of carnage because of the example of Muhammad himself, as well as other *conflicting* passages in the Islamic holy books. In other words, those who choose to interpret the teachings of Islam as a religion of peace have a rational basis for doing so, but so too do radical groups for their understanding; they have a rational, textual, and historical basis for engaging in *jihad* as a form of violence against other Muslims and non-Muslims.

If Christians glibly lump all Muslims together and say Islam is simply a religion of violence, they are dismantling one of the best arguments they can bring forth against Islam: that the inconsistency of Islamic teachings is proof *against* its divine origin. Thus, Christians would do well to embrace the reality of peaceful Muslims, as well as radical Muslims—to point out that such contradiction among the so-called words of God is a telling sign that their holy books are not of divine origin. When God speaks, He does so consistently, and the inconsistency in the *Qur'an* and *Hadith* are telling.

But setting all of that aside, supporters of Islam would point out that it has a rich tradition in its cultural and intellectual history. The Muslim world has produced many philosophers and scientist throughout its existence. Islam, therefore, is to be taken seriously, as a serious systematic faith, though it challenges the Christian faith. Islam is a challenge to the Christian faith because it has so many disturbing facets.

Islam oppresses women in countries where it is practiced and serves as the basis for its governing bodies of law. This oppression is not always equally show, but it can—and has—resulted in a number of on-going and horrific practices from female genital mutilation and honor killings to gang rapes and stonings (for rape victims and homosexuals), in the most several cases. Less oppressive examples include beatings for being "disobedient" wives or being forced and wearing head and body coverings to denying women education and driving privileges, to name just a few.[2]

Non-western Muslims are not viewed as joyful people. Law and tradition dictate their culture to a point that laughter is taken seriously. No one is allowed to say anything humorous about sex, religion, or politics.

Muslims express antipathy towards art. They do not hesitate to destroy ancient images they disapprove of.

Muslims agitate for Armageddon, as they await their Twelfth Iman.

Muslims behead people for engaging in homosexuality, being an infidel, or even being the form of Muslim. An "infidel" is defined as a person who does not believe in Allah, or that Muhammed is his prophet. Muslims kill homosexuals and infidels by throwing them off roof tops or drowning them in cages.[3]

---

[2] See http://www.heraldsun.com.au/blogs/andrew-bolt/muslim-women-explain-how-to-beat-women/news-story/21b6d0446003b9b55a7669c40979d904 (accessed July 8, 2017).

[3] The examples are numerous, but here are just two. Max Bearak and Darla Cameron, "Here are the 10 Countries Where Homosexuality may be Punished by Death," *Washing Post*, June 16, 2016 (accessed June 25, 2017). Also, John Hall, "Sickening new ISIS video shows caged prisoners lowered into a swimming pool and drowned," *Daily Mail*, June 23, 2015 (accessed June 25, 2017).

Muslims insist on conformity under penalty of death. After all, the very word *Islam*, means, "to submit." The harshness of Islam is appalling to Christians. There is little love.

There are four main contentions between the faith of Islam and Christianity.

First, Islam challenges the Christian faith about its view of God. Under Islam, the Fatherhood of God is rejected. There is no intimacy with God to a Muslim. Under Islam, the Trinity is vehemently opposed. For fourteen hundred years, Muslims have insisted that there is one God (that God is unitarian), and that Christians have been misled by teaching that Jesus is part of the Trinity.

Second, Islam challenges the Christian faith about its view of Man. Under Islam, the doctrine of the total depravity of man is rejected. The Christian faith, however, teaches that man is born in sin. "Behold, I was brought forth in iniquity, And in sin my mother conceived me" (Psa. 51:5). The vast majority of people believe that individuals are born basically good. While some people may do wrong, the innate goodness of a person is preferred to the idea of that every facet of the soul has been touched by sin, the will, the emotions, and the intellect. The Muslim is part of this vast majority.

Third, under Islam, the doctrine of salvation by grace, through faith alone in the substitutionary work of Christ, is rejected. Muslims reject the idea that because of the death of Christ on the Cross there is any hope of salvation through a Divine imputation of the righteousness of Christ to believer, and the imputation of sin to the Savior. The Muslim believes that every person is responsible for their own actions, and therefore for their own salvation. Each person will go before the divine scales to see if the good deeds outweigh the evil ones. Nobody else can pay for the personal sins of another. Islam challenges the Christian faith about its view of Christ. Under Islam, the death by crucifixion of Christ on the Cross is rejected. Under Islam, the deity of Christ is rejected. A Muslim will insist that Jesus never claimed to be divine. In contrast, the Jews understood the claims of Christ to be equal with God, and took up stones to kill Him for saying such a thing (John 8:59; 10:31).

> "Then the Jews surrounded Him and said to Him, 'How long do You keep us in doubt? If You are the Christ, tell us plainly.'
>
> [25] Jesus answered them, 'I told you, and you do not believe. The works that I do in My Father's name, they bear witness of Me. [26] But you do not believe, because you are not of My sheep, as I said to you. [27] My sheep hear My voice, and I know them, and they follow Me. [28] And I give them eternal life, and they shall never perish; neither shall anyone snatch them out of My hand. [29] My Father, who has given *them* to Me, is greater than all; and no one is able to snatch *them* out of My Father's hand. [30] I and *My* Father are one.'
>
> [31] Then the Jews took up stones again to stone Him. [32] Jesus answered them, 'Many good works I have shown you from My Father. For which of those works do you stone Me?'

[33] The Jews answered Him, saying, 'For a good work we do not stone You, but for blasphemy, and because You, being a Man, make Yourself God.'"

In contrast to Jews and Muslims, Christians affirm the divinity of Christ because of what Jesus said about Himself, and because of the teaching of the Bible as a whole, which is believed to be inspired. Therefore, Christians believe that, "In the beginning was the Word, and the Word was with God, and the Word was God . . . who were born, not of blood, nor of the will of the flesh, nor of the will of man, but of God" (John 1:1, 13).

Fourth, Islam challenges the Christian faith about its view of the Bible. Under Islam, Muslims reject the authenticity of the Bible as we possess it today. They insist that the transmission of the texts over the centuries has become utterly corrupted and cannot be considered a trustworthy source regarding the life and teachings of Jesus. (Of course, this is never demonstrated; it is merely assumed to be true). Under Islam, Muslims reject the authority of the Bible, to embrace the *Qur'an*. The theological challenges that come from the Muslim community also come from other groups as well, which helps to explain why Muslims can easily reject Christianity.

The matter is compounded when Christian writers, and theologians, also question the basic tenants of the faith. For example, the doctrine of the Trinity was attacked by Immanuel Kant, when he said that the doctrine of the Trinity provides nothing of practical value. Thomas Jefferson wrote,

"When we shall have done away the incomprehensible jargon of the Trinitarian arithmetic, that three are one, and one is three; when we shall have knocked down the artificial scaffolding, reared to mask from view the simple structure of Jesus; when, in short, we shall have unlearned everything which has been taught since His day, and got back to the pure and simple doctrines He inculcated, we shall then be truly and worthily His disciples; and my opinion is that if nothing had ever been added to what flowed purely from His lips, the whole world would at this day have been Christian."

The Christian writer, Dorothy Sawyer quipped, "The Father is incomprehensible; the Son is incomprehensible; the whole thing is inscrutable."

The secular consensus seems to be that the doctrine of the Trinity is something put in by theologians to make God more difficult to understand, and that it has no practical value for everyday life. The Muslim community picks up on these arguments and advances them as well.

The historic Christian position is that while the Trinity is indeed incomprehensible, and to study it might cause a person to lose their concentration, to deny the doctrine of the Trinity is to lose one's soul.

The growth of Islam has a great appeal to people in every nation, because it presents itself a simple and rational religion. Muslims believe that Islam is a viable alternative to the Christian religion that is filled with mysteries, and concepts, that are incomprehensible, based on faith.

Many Christians do not even understand the basis of their own faith, and so cannot answer any challenges to it. The Muslims take advantage of this fact, and exploit it to teach that Islam is a simple religion that even a child can understand. The Crescent is a great challenge to the Cross.

FOUR

Islam and the Fatherhood of God

Jesus taught people to pray to God as Father. "In this manner, therefore, pray: Our Father in heaven, Hallowed be Your name. ¹⁰ Your kingdom come. Your will be done On earth as *it is* in heaven. ¹¹ Give us this day our daily bread" (Matt. 6:9–11). The Christian feels privileged to talk to God in such intimacy. We have not received the spirit of bondage again to fear; but we have received the Spirit of adoption, whereby we cry, "Abba, Father" (Rom. 8:15).

When Christians share with Muslims the biblical concept of the Fatherhood of God, many may not realize that to Muslims such is a terrible message, and for this reason: it sounds blasphemous. The *Qur'an* sets the stage for the Muslim understanding of God.

> "Say: 'He, Allah, is One,' 'Allah, the Eternal, 'He begets not, nor is He begotten, 'And there is none like unto Him'" (Surah 112:1–4).

These four verses are cited in prayer each day by millions of Muslims around the world.

Another important Surah for a devout Muslim is Surah 19:35.

"It is not [befitting] for Allah to take a son; exalted is He! When He decrees an affair, He only says to it, 'Be,' and it is."

Muslims believe that begetting a son is a physical act, depending on the animal need of human nature. God Most High is independent of all needs, and so it is derogatory to Him to contribute to Him such an act. It is merely a relic of material and anthromorphic superstition, and is unworthy of Him. To talk about God as Father, for a Muslim, is to talk about sexual relations, and therefore to attribute something that is not right to God.

Ironically, there are many truths about God which Christians and Muslims agree on. Here are a few:

- God is one.
- God is good.
- God is just.
- God is sovereign.
- God rules.
- God forgives.
- God has sent prophets.
- God has given revelation.

However, there are fundamental differences. These differences, when they relate to God, are based, in part, on the Muslims understanding of the Fatherhood of God in material and physical terms, and not in the figurative usage of language which is conveyed in Holy Scripture.

There are many figurative images of God in the Bible.

- God is our Father.
- God is our Shepherd.
- God is our Rock.
- God is our Protector under whose "wings" we abide. The psalmist says, "He shall cover you with His feathers, And under His wings you shall take refuge;" (Psa. 91:4).
- God is a Faithful Husband who goes after His unfaithful wife Israel, in the book of Hosea.

There are many tender images of God in His relationship to humanity. The *Qur'an* perverts these images by pressing for literalism, when the language is figurative. Tragically, Islam does not allow for any intimacy between humans and God. Therefore, the Christian should be aware about the Muslim understanding of phrases, such as "son of God," or, God as "our Father."

Of course, Orthodox Christianity rejects, and repudiates any idea of a crass materialism, whereby God sexually engages with His creation, like the Greeks, and Romans believed about their gods in their mythology.

In Christian theology, the Sonship of Christ is spoken of in terms of eternal generation, not physical procreation. Jesus also spoke of God the Father in terms of subordination to the will of the Father.

In Christian theology, the sonship of man to God is based on adoption, whereby we can call Him "Abba, Father." Christians are not God's children by nature, but by adoption. We are like Mephibosheth, in the family of Saul, who was taken in by David, and treated with mercy and grace.

The conclusion, is that the Muslim religion does not have any way to be united to God in a filial way, and so is an impoverished religion. Only the Christian can say, "Behold what manner of love the Father has bestowed on us, that we should be called children of God! Therefore the world does not know us, because it did not know Him" (1 John 3:1).

FIVE

Islam and the Doctrine of the Trinity

T he *Qur'an* is filled with passages declaring that God is One. And by "One," they mean in the Unitarian sense, in the understanding that one Being is shared by only one Person. Therefore, they cannot conceive of the Christian doctrine of One God whose Being is one in essence but three in persons: Father, Son, and Holy Spirit. Muslims believe that the gift of Islam is the gift to the world of pure (unitarian) monotheism. On this point, the Muslims are arrogantly, and factually, wrong, for Judaism and Christianity are passionately committed to monotheism. Both world religions predate Islam. The devout Muslim believes that Christianity has been corrupted by embracing the Trinity. The *Qur'an* is the basis of this belief.

> "O People of the Scripture, do not commit excess in
> your religion or say about Allah except the truth. The
> Messiah, Jesus, the son of Mary, was but a messenger of
> Allah and His word which He directed to Mary and a
> soul [created at a command] from Him. So believe in
> Allah and His messengers. And do not say, 'Three';
> desist—it is better for you. Indeed, Allah is but one God.

Exalted is He above having a son. To Him belongs whatever is in the heavens and whatever is on the earth. And sufficient is Allah as Disposer of affairs" (Surah 4:171).

"The Messiah, son of Mary, was no more than a Messenger before whom many Messengers have passed away; and his mother adhered wholly to truthfulness, and they both ate food (as other mortals do). See how We make Our signs clear to them; and see where they are turning away!" (Surah 5:75).

"In these few words the Christian doctrine of the divinity of Christ is repudiated. The nature of the Messiah is clear from the indications given here; he was merely a human being. He was one born from the womb of a woman, who had a known genealogy, who possessed a physical body, who was subject to all the limitations of a human being, and who had all the attributes characteristic of human beings. He slept, ate, felt the discomfort of heat and cold, and was so human that he was even put to the test by Satan. How could any reasonable person believe that such a being was either God or a partner, or associate of God in His godhead? But the Christians continue to insist on the divinity of the Messiah, whose life has been portrayed in their own Scriptures as that of a human. The fact of the matter is that they do not believe at all in the historical Messiah. They have woven a Messiah out of their imagination and have deified that imaginary being."[1] (Understanding the Qur'an)

The *Qur'an* goes on to teach, that, in the Day of Judgment, a conversation will take place between Jesus and God whereby Jesus declares He did not invite anyone to worship Him, or Mary, as gods, beside Allah.

> "And imagine when thereafter Allah will say: 'Jesus, son of Mary, did you say to people: "Take me and my mother for gods beside Allah?" and he will answer: 'Glory to You! It was not for me to say what I had no right to. Had I said so, You would surely have known it. You know all what is within my mind whereas I do not know what is within Yours. You, indeed You, know fully all that is beyond the reach of human perception'" (Surah 5:116).

The Muslims are right to reject any form of Mariology, but they are misguided in rejecting Christ as divine.

While the Christian Doctrine of the Trinity is complex, it is not incomprehensible. While the Doctrine of the Trinity contains a paradox, it does not contain a contradiction. While the Doctrine of the Trinity is a great mystery, it is not beyond human comprehension. The Trinity emphasis a Tri-unity, with the emphasis being on Unity. A distinction must be made in three categories: contradiction, paradox, and mystery.

---

[1] Mawdudi, *Towards Understanding the Qur'an*, 173.

Contradiction. Aristotle taught the Law of Non-Contradiction. Said Aristotle, something cannot *be* what it is, and *not be* what it is, at the same time, and in the same relationship. That would be a contradiction. For example, a circle cannot both be a circle and not be a circle as the same time; in other words, a circle cannot both be a circle and a square.

Paradox. The root of this word, *dox*, comes from a word which means, "to seem," "to think," or "to appear." The early teachers of Docetism taught that Jesus did not have a true body, but only appeared or seemed to have one. John had to write,

> "By this you know the Spirit of God: Every spirit that confesses that Jesus Christ has come in the flesh is of God, ³ and every spirit that does not confess that Jesus Christ has come in the flesh is not of God. And this is the *spirit* of the Antichrist, which you have heard was coming, and is now already in the world" (1 John 4:2–3).

A paradox means that something seems to be a contradiction when it is placed along something, but it is not. A paradox is not a contradiction. It is an apparent contradiction. Jesus said His followers have to become a slave, in one sense, in order to be free, in another sense. The Christian rises to heaven when he is bowed low in prayer. To die to self, is to live forever.

Mystery. While God in His essence is incomprehensible, this does not mean God is completely unknowable. There are many passages in the Bible which teach what God is. While no man has an exhaustive and comprehensive knowledge of God in His fullness, God has revealed many facets of His essence to man. To say that God is infinite in understanding is something beyond our comprehension and so remains a mystery to us.

This should not be a problem. There are many truths that are affirmed in science that the mind has yet to penetrate fully. Gravity, motion, and subatomic particles are not fully understood. Just because something remains a mystery because it is not fully understood, does not mean it is contradictory, nonsensical, or absurd.

To personalize, the conclusion is this. I do not understand mysteries. I do not understand contradictions. Contradictions should be challenged no matter who expresses them. Dr. R. C. Sproul tells about one of his college professors who taught, "God is absolutely immutable in His being; God is absolutely mutable in His being." Said Dr. R. C. Sproul, "The professor was teaching something that is contradictory and irrational. What he said was a clear contradiction, not a mystery."

A mystery is not inherently unintelligible. A mystery does not violate the Law of Non-Contradiction. The essence of God remains a mystery and incomprehensible, but there is nothing contradictory about it.

The Church has always taught that God is one in essence, but three in persons. A person has will, emotion, and intellect. God the Father has these characteristics. God the Son has these characteristics. God the Holy Spirit has these characteristics.

Whatever divine attribute is ascribed to God the Father, is ascribed in Scripture to God the Son, and God the Holy Spirit. While there are distinctions among the Persons of the Trinity, there is no distinction in the essence or Being of God. God is one single being. God is one in Being, but three in persons. The plurality is in a different category than the category of Being.

The Church speaks of there being subsistence within God so that the Son is subordinate to the Father.

So, a person can say they do not believe in the Trinity. That is their right. What a person cannot say is that the formula for the Trinity breaks the Law of Non-Contradiction. It does not. The Doctrine of the Trinity is not irrational. It is not contradictory. It is a mystery.

The Church has taught that the distinctions within the Godhead are real, but they are not essential to God's Being in His essence. The essence of the Son, the essence of the Holy Spirit, is the same as the essence of the Father. There is only one Being. But within the Being of God's subsistence, there are three persona, but they are not distinguished from His essence. God is immutable, God is eternal. This is a distinction without division.

By way of practical application, if Jesus is LORD, and He is, then His commandments are not mere suggestions, but binding. Jesus is not simply an insightful moral Teacher. He is very God of very God. One day, every knee shall bow before Him and every tongue shall confess that He is LORD.

Again, by way of practical application, it is important to embrace the Holy Spirit as very God of very God because it is the Holy Spirit who enables the believer to remember, and keep, the teaching of Jesus, and to pray appropriately.

Christian, do not doubt the Biblical doctrine of the Trinity.

SIX

Islam and the Deity of Christ

Since the *Qur'an* denies the doctrine of the Trinity, it, therefore, also denies the deity of Christ. Here are a few passages confirming this.

> "They have certainly disbelieved who say, 'Allah is the third of three.' And there is no god except one God. And if they do not desist from what they are saying, there will surely afflict the disbelievers among them a painful punishment" (Surah 5:74).
>
> [75] The Messiah, son of Mary, was not but a messenger; [other] messengers have passed on before him. And his mother was a supporter of truth. They both use to eat food. Look how we make clear to them the signs; then look how they are deluded.
>
> [76] Say, 'Do you worship besides Allah that which holds for you no [power of] harm or benefit while it is Allah who is the Hearing, the Knowing?'
>
> [77] Say, 'O People of the Scripture, do not exceed limits in your religion beyond the truth and do not follow the inclinations of a people who had gone astray before and

misled many and have strayed from the soundness of the way.'

[78] Cursed were those who disbelieved among the Children of Israel by the tongue of David and of Jesus, the son of Mary. That was because they disobeyed and [habitually] transgressed" (Surah 5:74–78).

Christianity teaches that believing in Jesus as the Son of God is the key to eternal life. Islam teaches that to believe in Jesus as the Son of God is to be placed under the curse of Allah. It is the unpardonable sin. According to the *Qur'an*, Allah will forgive any sin *except* the sin of attributing a partner to Allah. Muslims are offended that Christians have exalted a human prophet to the same level as God. During His ministry, the Jews were just as offended at Jesus. "The Jews answered Him, saying, 'For a good work we do not stone You, but for blasphemy, and because You, being a Man, make Yourself God'" (John 10:33).

Modern Muslims find an ally with the Jews against the divinity of Christ, and they have found an ally with liberal Bible scholars who also deny the deity of Christ.

Another argument Muslims use to disprove the deity of Christ, is to appeal to the statements of Jesus, in which He confessed His limitations.

"But of that day and hour no one knows, not even the angels of heaven, but My Father only" (Matt. 24:36)

"So Jesus said to him, 'Why do you call Me good? No one *is* good but One, *that is*, God'" (Mark 10:18).

The Muslim charges the Christian with elevating Jesus to being God, which is a sin to be repented of.

In response, it must be noted, that while many people contend that both Islam and Christianity are equal, nothing is further from the truth. It is illogical to think that both are true, when they are diametrically opposed to each on the matter of sin, salvation, the atonement, the death of Christ, His resurrection, and His divinity. There are radical differences between Islam and Christianity.

Of course, if both religions were false, then it could be said they were equal. However, it is impossible for Christianity, the greatest moral religion in the world, to be built upon a lie. If Christ is not risen from the dead, then Christianity is a lie. However, Christ is risen from the dead, which is a well-attested historical event. In fact, Christianity is the only religion that invites its followers to base its faith, not only on the words of its founders, but upon a verifiable historical event. The Buddhist says, "Believe what Buddha taught." The Muslim says, "Believe what Muhammad proclaimed." Christianity says, "Look at the empty tomb and believe that Christ is who He claimed to be, the Son of the Living God."

In response to the Muslim uniting with liberal scholars, who attack the divinity of Christ, it should be noted that those who profess to be Christian, but deny the divinity of Christ, are imposters. They are not Christians. They have no right to the title. They are not the sheep of the Lord's flock. Liberal theologians who deny the death burial and resurrection of Jesus are nothing more than unbelievers. Because they are heretical in their belief, they study and operate outside the kingdom of God.

In the fourth century, when the deity of Christ was disputed, the controversy ended at the Council of Nicaea in A.D. 325. In the fifth century, when the deity of Christ was disputed, the controversy ended at the Council of Chalcedon in A.D. 451. In the nineteenth and twentieth century, when the deity of Christ was disputed, the controversy was challenged by the rise of Fundamentalism, which found roots in the Niagara Bible Conferences held between 1878 and 1897.

In response to the Muslims uniting with Jewish culture, to attack the divinity of Jesus, that is not a surprise. The Jews in the days of Jesus, rejected Him as their Messiah, and crucified Him in ignorance.

> "Yet now, brethren, I know that you did *it* in ignorance, as *did* also your rulers. [18] But those things which God foretold by the mouth of all His prophets, that the Christ would suffer, He has thus fulfilled. [19] Repent therefore and be converted, that your sins may be blotted out, so that times of refreshing may come from the presence of the Lord" (Acts 3:17–19).

It should also be noted, that not all Jews reject Jesus as the Messiah, and as "very God of very God." There are hundreds upon thousands of converted Jews. Many are called "Messianic Jews" because they believe in Jesus as the promised Messiah and have been baptized into His name.

In response to the claim that Jesus never claimed to be God, and that the Bible teaches He was not God, the answer is this.

Read the whole counsel of God. Read the entire Bible, and a different conclusion will be drawn.

If there is one truth the New Testament contends for, it is the divinity of Jesus. The confession of the early church, as found in Scripture, is that Jesus Christ was God, "manifested in the flesh, Justified in the Spirit, Seen by angels, Preached among the Gentiles, Believed on in the world, Received up in glory" (1 Tim. 3:16).

When Jesus asked the rich young ruler why he called Him good, Jesus was not saying the young man should not call Him God, or good. He was just asking if the young man knew what He was saying. The young man had a superficial understanding of what it meant to be "good." He had an understanding of goodness that Muslims later embraced—a scale of divine justice that weighs the so-called good deeds against the bad ones. So Jesus gave the young man a test, which he failed. The Lord proved the man did not begin to understand what true goodness was, or what the commandments of God entailed.

If Jesus was not claiming to be God, He was also claiming not to be good, and if that were true He disqualified Himself from being the Pascal Lamb which had to be without blemish. All of that is reading too much into the answer of Jesus.

A possible inference is not a necessary inference. The whole of the New Testament declares that Jesus is God manifested in the flesh. Jesus is good in His humanity. Jesus is the perfect Paschal Lamb able to take away the sin of the world. Jesus identified Himself with sinlessness, not sinfulness.

Muslims find it difficult, if not impossible, to believe that the Infinite God could become finite. A conservative Christian would, in fact agree, that it is impossible for the Infinite to become finite. What is not impossible to believe, is that, in the Person of Jesus Christ, the Son of God could become incarnate, so that in Jesus, there is One person with two natures. The human nature of Jesus was not divine, nor was the divine nature of Jesus human.

What the church maintains is that Jesus had both a human nature, so that He was true humanity, with all of the limitations that a human has, but He was also divine, with all the attributes ascribed to God the Father. This union of the human and the divine nature, is called the "hypostatic union." The human nature of Jesus was not omniscient, but His divine nature was. So, Jesus could say that He did not know when a certain event would occur. But, then, Jesus could also say, from His divine nature what would happen 40 years hence to the city of Jerusalem. His prophetic words are recorded in Matthew 24, Mark 13, and Luke 21. While it is a great mystery, it is not illogical to believe. Jesus did claim to be deity, and the Jews of His day understood what He was saying.

Jesus claimed to be Lord of the Sabbath. He claimed the right to forgive sins.

> "'Which is easier, to say, "Your sins are forgiven you," or to say, "Rise up and walk?"' [24] But that you may know that the Son of Man has power on earth to forgive sins'—He said to the man who was paralyzed, 'I say to you, arise, take up your bed, and go to your house'" (Luke 5:23–24).

Jesus claimed to be deity when He took for Himself the divine phrase, *ego eimi*, I AM—The divine name of God, YAHWEH. Jesus consciously used the language reserved for God in the Old Testament.

> "And Jesus said to them, 'I am the bread of life. He who comes to Me shall never hunger, and he who believes in Me shall never thirst'" (John 6:35).

> "Then Jesus spoke to them again, saying, 'I am the light of the world. He who follows Me shall not walk in darkness, but have the light of life'" (John 8:12).

> "Jesus said to them, 'Most assuredly, I say to you, before Abraham was, I AM'" (John 8:58).

> "I am the door. If anyone enters by Me, he will be saved, and will go in and out and find pasture" (John 10:9).

> "I am the good shepherd. The good shepherd gives His life for the sheep" (John 10:11).

> "Jesus said to her, 'I am the resurrection and the life. He who believes in Me, though he may die, he shall live'" (John 11:25).

> "Jesus said to him, 'I am the way, the truth, and the life. No one comes to the Father except through Me'" (John 14:6).

"I am the true vine, and My Father is the vinedresser" (John 15:1).

Jesus claimed to be deity when He referred to Himself as the Son of Man nearly eighty times in the Gospel narratives. This was a term ascribed to a heavenly being in the book of Daniel. "I was watching in the night visions, And behold, *One* like the Son of Man, Coming with the clouds of heaven! He came to the Ancient of Days, And they brought Him near before Him" (Dan. 7:13).

The New Testament is filled with references to Jesus Christ as deity, if only one is willing to find them and honestly accept them when they appear in Scripture.

What Muslims must come to understand is that a distinction must be made between the *human* nature of Jesus and His *divine* nature. The two natures can be distinguished, but they cannot be separated from the person of Christ. Muslims mock, and ask, "Why did God pray to God?" "Why did God cry out to God?" Such question demonstrate, not only a fundamental misunderstanding of the natures of Jesus, but of the biblical revelation of the Triune God. The Christian does not mock, but recognizes that Jesus was truly human, and so He prayed, and was thirsty, and cried. Jesus was deity, and so had power to heal, forgive sins, and exercise His sovereignty over nature. Christians affirm the humanity of Jesus and also the deity of Christ. If Jesus was not truly and fully human, He could not make atonement for our sins; if He was not truly and fully divine, He would be insufficient to meet the demand necessary to satisfy the judgment.

Only God could fully and completely make payment for sin. For this reason, He is the most unique Person in the universe.

SEVEN

Islam and Man the Sinner

There are four major areas of conflict between Islam and Christianity: the doctrine of God, the doctrine of man, the doctrine of Jesus Christ, and the doctrine of Scripture. According to the *Qur'an*, God created man in order to serve Him. There is a Master to servant relationship between God and man, which does not invite intimacy.

In contrast, Christianity invites individuals to call God, Father. "In this manner, therefore, pray: Our Father in heaven, hallowed be Your name" (Matt. 6:9). The Christian can be even more intimate with God, and call him "Papa." "For you did not receive the spirit of bondage again to fear, but you received the Spirit of adoption by whom we cry out, 'Abba, Father.' The Spirit Himself bears witness with our spirit that we are children of God" (Rom. 8:15–16).

According to the *Qur'an*, though God created Adam and Eve to serve Him, they sinned. Nevertheless, in grace, throughout history, God sent prophets to guide individuals to the straight path of worshipping the one God, and doing good deeds while living for the Day of Judgment. The story of the Fall in the *Qur'an*, is similar to the story of the Fall in the Bible.

> "And We said, 'O Adam, dwell, you and your wife, in Paradise and eat therefrom in [ease and] abundance from wherever you will. But do not approach this tree, lest you be among the wrongdoers.'
>
> But Satan caused them to slip out of it and removed them from that [condition] in which they had been. And We said, 'Go down, [all of you], as enemies to one another, and you will have upon the earth a place of settlement and provision for a time.'
>
> Then Adam received from his Lord [some] words, and He accepted his repentance. Indeed, it is He who is the Accepting of repentance, the Merciful" (Surah 2:35).

Though created in a state of Paradise, Adam and Eve were expelled from Paradise to earth. Adam sinned, God forgave Him, and then Adam became the first Prophet. (A Prophet in the Islamic faith is more pure and righteous than an ordinary man.)

The important point is that the sin of Adam had no consequence for his posterity. The Fall is seen as a continuous manifestation of evil, or simply, disobedience to God's will. Adam's disobedience was due to ignorance and weakness of will.

In the Bible, Adam knew what he was doing, he deliberately ate of the forbidden fruit, and he strongly willed to do wrong. In Islam, there is no original sin passed on to others, so that individuals are not born physically alive, but spiritually dead, even though the Bible teaches this concept. "Therefore, just as through one man sin entered the world, and death through sin, and thus death spread to all men, because all sinned" (Rom. 5:12).

In Islam, men are not sinful by nature. Men are weak-willed, arrogant, ungrateful, but are not essentially fallen, or sinful. People are born innocent. Every individual makes themselves guilty by a deed which is blameworthy. Islam does not believe in original sin.

The practical consequence of this is that the Muslim does not want to be told he is a sinner in need of salvation. In this, the Muslim finds harmony with the thinking of many in the Western world, where people think they are innately good. Individuals do not want to be told they are weak, fallen creatures, in need of help.

Islam pretends to give dignity to individuals by telling them to raise themselves up, and live as God intended them to live. Individuals can do it. They can take responsibility for themselves, and clean up their society.

There are two major schools of theological thinking within Christianity that would applaud the Islamic view of man's self-dignity, worth, and ability. There is the Pelagian school of thought. There is the semi-Pelagian school of thought.

In contrast to Pelagianism, Semi-Pelagianism, and Islam, and their view of man's innate goodness, dignity, worth, and ability, is the Augustinian School of Thought, which teaches just the opposite. The Bible does not teach that fallen man is noble, dignified, and able to please God.

The Bible says that man by nature is a sinner who does not do good, and does not seek after God. "As it is written: 'There is none righteous, no, not one; There is none who understands; There is none who seeks after God. They have all turned aside; They have together become unprofitable; There is none who does good, no, not one'" (Rom. 3:10–12).

Pelagianism, along with Islam, denies Original Sin. The fifth-century, British monk, Pelagius, took the position that Adam's sin affected Adam—and only Adam. His sin did not have the power to distort the basic composition in man. The Muslims agree, and reject the doctrine of Original Sin.

In the Church, the teaching of Pelagius was condemned, and deemed heretical. In the 16th century the error of Pelagius was resurrected in the Socinian controversy, and again in the 19th century with the rise of Charles Finney. Socinianism refers to a system of doctrine named for the Italian, Fausto Sozzini (1539–1604), who ministered in Poland in the Minor Reformed Church. He rejected the doctrine of the Trinity, the doctrine of Original Sin, and the doctrine of the divinity of Christ. The propitiatory view of the atonement was also rejected. God's omniscience was limited to what was a necessary truth in the future, or what would definitely happen, and did not apply to what might happen. This view was embraced in order to protect man's free will. In all of these points, the theology of Islam is comfortable.

Islam believes that man is born innocent, but is corrupted by society. That of course begs the question, for how did society become so corrupt? Why is all of humanity blameworthy? "Because all have sinned and come short of the glory of God" (Rom. 3:23), is the Biblical answer.

The fundamental problem in wrestling with the dark side of man is a distorted view of God. Humans look at other humans, and feel justified with exalting in their self-esteem. But then, such individuals fail to look at the majesty and holiness of God, and compare themselves to Him. If they did, they would cry out, "I am an unclean person, and I dwell in the midst of unclean people" (Isa. 6:5).

In contrast to man's uncleanness, is the holiness of God. However, in the entire *Qur'an*, the quality of God being holy is only mentioned twice. In the Bible, the text of Isaiah 6:3 mentions God's holiness more times than in all the *Qur'an*. This is significant.

When this facet of the character of God is diminished, the personal standard of holiness, and righteousness, is diminished with it. This is what the Muslims do. They believe their god, Allah, tells them to kill infidels, including women, and children. Their god is a blood-thirty god, whose appetite for human violence is never abated. As a result, a devout Muslim who engages in *jihad*, can exalt himself as a superior person who is devoted to Allah. Such Muslims address themselves as nothing less than demi-gods.

The Bible teaches that those who will judge themselves, by themselves are not wise (2 Cor. 10:12).

The Muslim that would be wise, and righteous, must bow to the Lordship of Christ, who taught His followers, saying,

> "But I say to you, love your enemies, bless those who curse you, do good to those who hate you, and pray for those who spitefully use you and persecute you, [45] that you may be sons of your Father in heaven; for He makes

His sun rise on the evil and on the good, and sends rain
on the just and on the unjust" (Matt. 5:44–45).

Though the Muslim does not believe there is anything to be redeemed from, the Christian must continue to be faithful, by proclaiming the truth of the ruin of man by the fall, the redemption of man by Christ, and the regeneration of the heart by the Holy Spirit.

The Christian message is in violent conflict with the message of the Muslim faith. Nevertheless, let God be true and every man a liar that opposes God's truth (Rom. 3:4).

In the end, the conflict will be settled by God Himself as the mouths of the false witnesses are silenced, and a new heart is given to those who are the heirs of salvation.

Muslims like to teach that God has revealed His will, and that is enough. The Bible teaches that God has revealed His will and His character, and that is important, for God's character is one of kindness, mercy, and holiness. "Be holy, for I am holy" (1 Pet. 1:16), is the royal command and the will of God, based on the character of God.

It is important to remember, that we do not all believe in the same God. The god, Allah, is different from the Biblical God of Abraham, Isaac, and Jacob, who is holy, just, and good. In the person of Jesus Christ, God has manifested Himself in the flesh in order to be the Savior of those who, by faith, embrace His gift of eternal life through Jesus Christ. We plead with our Muslim friends to come to Christ. Lay down your weapons of warfare against Christians. Love Jesus. Love the brethren. Be honest about your own sinful nature. Ask for a new heart and for forgiveness of sin.

EIGHT

Islam and the Atonement

I t is instructive to note that the *Qur'an* mentions Jesus on several occasions. The *Qur'an* calls Jesus the Messiah. He is called a Word from Allah, and, the Spirit of Allah. The *Qur'an* claims Jesus was born of the virgin, Mary. Jesus did many miracles, including raising people from the dead. Jesus is alive today, according to the *Qur'an*. According to the Sunni Muslims, Jesus will someday return. He is the Messenger of Allah.

Muslims assume they know all the important truths concerning Jesus. They already honor Him as one of the greatest prophets. He is second to Muhammed. Jesus has a special place in the hearts of many Muslims.

One manifest problem with the Islamic understanding of Jesus, however, is that the *Qur'an* denies He died on the Cross. The argument is made that Jesus only swooned on the Cross, was refreshed in the tomb, and walked away from it as a man, not as the resurrected Son of the living God. Therein is the problem.

In contrast, the death, burial, and bodily resurrection of Jesus from the dead, is the central core of the Christian faith. Without the resurrection, there is no atonement. Without the atonement, the sufferings of Christ are tragic, but not redemptive in nature.

"Moreover, brethren, I declare to you the gospel which I preached to you, which also you received and in which you stand, 2 by which also you are saved, if you hold fast that word which I preached to you—unless you believed in vain.

3 For I delivered to you first of all that which I also received: that Christ died for our sins according to the Scriptures, 4 and that He was buried, and that He rose again the third day according to the Scriptures, 5 and that He was seen by Cephas, then by the twelve. 6 After that He was seen by over five hundred brethren at once, of whom the greater part remain to the present, but some have fallen asleep. 7 After that He was seen by James, then by all the apostles. 8 Then last of all He was seen by me also, as by one born out of due time.

9 For I am the least of the apostles, who am not worthy to be called an apostle, because I persecuted the church of God. 10 But by the grace of God I am what I am, and His grace toward me was not in vain; but I labored more abundantly than they all, yet not I, but the grace of God *which was* with me. 11 Therefore, whether *it was* I or they, so we preach and so you believed.

12 Now if Christ is preached that He has been raised from the dead, how do some among you say that there is no resurrection of the dead? 13 But if there is no resurrection of the dead, then Christ is not risen. 14 And

if Christ is not risen, then our preaching *is* empty and your faith *is* also empty. ¹⁵ Yes, and we are found false witnesses of God, because we have testified of God that He raised up Christ, whom He did not raise up—if in fact the dead do not rise. ¹⁶ For if *the* dead do not rise, then Christ is not risen. ¹⁷ And if Christ is not risen, your faith *is* futile; you are still in your sins! ¹⁸ Then also those who have fallen asleep in Christ have perished. ¹⁹ If in this life only we have hope in Christ, we are of all men the most pitiable" (1 Cor. 15:1–19).

While a Muslim will read beautiful things about Jesus in the *Qur'an*, they deny the most fundamental truth about Him. Jesus is the Savior of all who believe because He is divine, and because He died on a tree. No, says the *Qur'an*, Jesus did not die.

"And [for] their saying, 'Indeed, we have killed the Messiah, Jesus, the son of Mary, the messenger of Allah.' And they did not kill him, nor did they crucify him; but [another] was made to resemble him to them. And indeed, those who differ over it are in doubt about it. They have no knowledge of it except the following of assumption. And they did not kill him, for certain.

Rather, Allah raised him to Himself. And ever is Allah Exalted in Might and Wise" (Surah 4:157–158).

According to the *Qur'an*, Allah was involved in some kind of a trickery, which led people to assume Jesus had been crucified, when He had not been put to death on a cross by the Jews.

In Islam, there is a denial of the historical death, burial, and resurrection of Jesus, because they do not believe a prophet of Allah could be so humiliated, and die such a shameful death. Allah would never allow his honored messengers to be treated like that.

Moreover, there was no need for Jesus to die for others, because each person is responsible for their own moral actions, and their own future destiny.

The Christian protests such a view in favor of the historical evidence of the death, burial, and resurrection of Christ. The Christian protests such a view of Jesus, because it takes away any hope of a covering, or atonement, for sin. The Christians sings:

"He paid a debt He did not owe.
    I owed a debt I could not pay.
I needed Someone to wash my sins away.
    And now I sing a brand new song,
'Amazing Grace,' (all day long)
    Christ Jesus paid a debt that I could never pay.

He paid a debt at Calvary,
    He cleansed my soul and made me free,
I'm glad that Jesus did all my sins erase;
    I now can sing a brand new song,
'Amazing Grace,' (all day long)
    Christ Jesus paid a debt that I could never pay.

You ask me why He paid the price,
    Why He would make the sacrifice
Why He would walk up that hill called Calvary

He loved me more than His own life
    O glorious day (He saved my life!)
My Jesus paid the debt that I could never pay.

One day He's coming back for me
    To live with Him eternally,
Won't it be glory to see Him on that day!
    I then will sing a brand new song,
'Amazing Grace,' (all day long)
    Christ Jesus paid a debt that I could never pay."

The Muslim is found to have a hopeless mindset, filled with contradictions. The Muslim will believe some things the Gospels teach about Jesus, and restate the Gospel teachings in the *Qur'an*, but will reject other teachings about Jesus from the Gospels.

It is this selective belief that leaves the Muslim in darkness and despair, without Christ, without eternal life, without hope, except in their own innate goodness. Their eternal future is built upon a house of sand. It is doomed to fall.

Instead of allowing a Gospel text to speak, a preconceived notion is given to the passage. When the Gospels speak about the death of Christ, the Muslim exercises a preconceived notion and says, "That could not have happened, because Allah would not allow His prophets to suffer."

Since the *Qur'an* teaches that Jesus is the Messiah, the Muslim would be wise to go back to the Old Testament, and notice afresh that the motif of the Messiah was that He would suffer. Since Jesus is the Messiah, He must suffer in order to fulfill prophesy.

What is needed is for the Muslim to abandon his preconceived notions, and embrace what the Holy Scripture actually says.

Jesus did come to suffer and die, despite the protests of Peter, who did not want the Messiah to suffer.

The Muslim basis his preconceived notion about what Allah would not allow, not on the Bible, but on the *Qur'an*. To a Muslim, the final word of divine revelation was given to Muhammed, not the Jews.

Therefore, if the *Qur'an* contradicts the Bible, and it does, then the Bible is in error, even though it was completed 500 years before Muhammed was born.

The Bible cannot just be dismissed arbitrarily. Nor can one part of the Bible be embraced as being truthful, and another part of the Bible be dismissed as untruthful. Either the historical documents found in the Bible are reliable, or they are not.

The Bible says that Jesus had a human nature. He did not seem to be man, as some claim, Jesus was true humanity. "And the Word became flesh and dwelt among us, and we beheld His glory, the glory as of the only begotten of the Father, full of grace and truth" (John 1:14)

The Bible says that Jesus died a violent death on the Cross. "Who Himself bore our sins in His own body on the tree, that we, having died to sins, might live for righteousness—by whose stripes you were healed" (1 Pet. 2:24)

The Bible says that Jesus arose again from the dead. And yet, no matter how much historical evidence is presented to the Muslim for the actual death of Jesus, His resurrection, and the accuracy of the Bible, their presuppositional position will not let them believe.

How then, does a person witness to a Muslim? The answer is simple. Preach Christ. Proclaim the gospel and pray that God the Holy Spirit will do what no human can do, and that is illuminate the soul, and change the heart, so that in the day of gospel hearing it wills to believe.

There are Christians who believe that if they present enough evidence to a Muslim, a Mormon, a skeptic, or a liberal, the evidence will demand a positive verdict. That is a false hope. "A man convinced against his will, is of the same opinion still." Only God can convert a soul. Only the Holy Spirit can give spiritual eyes to those who are spiritually blind. Salvation is of the Lord.

The heart of the unbeliever is so stubborn, and so wicked, it will emotionally deny what cannot be rationally denied. A billion Muslims deny the historical reality of the death and resurrection of Jesus, just like many people in the Western world deny the reality of the Holocaust.

There is a reason why Muslims want to deny the death of Christ and that is because of the meaning Christians give to the death of Christ.

In Christian theology, the death of Christ was atonement for sin. It is the atoning facet of the death of Christ which Muslims reject.

The Muslim does not believe atonement can be paid by someone else. The individual must pay their own debt. Therefore, a person must be their own savior. The Muslim actually thinks this is possible.

What the Muslim fails to distinguish, is the difference between a *pecuniary* debt and a *moral* debt. When there is a pecuniary debt, money will resolve the issue. When there is a moral debt, someone else must forgive the individual. Only God can forgive a moral debt. God's forgiveness can be extended, when His righteousness has been satisfied. Only Someone His equal can satisfy what is righteously demanded. That Someone is Jesus, the perfect Lamb of God, who taketh away the sin of the world.

The glory of the gospel, is that God accepts the payment of a Substitute, who willingly paid my moral debt. God extends His grace and mercy, but He is also just, for sin is punished.

There is more. The salvation of a sinner is not simply by the death of Jesus, but by the life of Jesus as well. There is a double transfer that takes place. The righteousness of Christ is transferred to me, while my unrighteousness, my moral debt, is transferred to Him. The life of Christ is transferred to me, while my death is transferred to Him by imputation.

Muslims may not like this, but God has a right to make this transaction. Christ stood in our stead, because we are incapable of redeeming ourselves.

The Muslim can face the justice of God, and be judged for his own righteousness, or he can stand, and be judged on the righteousness of Another, even Jesus.

Muslims forget, that the idea of atonement is not a Christian novelty, but a truth, taught in the Old Testament, in the book of Genesis, and in Leviticus. A moral life was to be lived, but a sacrifice had to be made.

It is the Muslim that has left the tradition of having an atonement for sin by a substitute. In the Jewish economy, that substitute was an animal. In the Christian economy, that substitute is Jesus.

Those who place their trust in Jesus shall be covered by His blood in the Day of Judgment and receive forgiveness of all sin.

NINE

Islam, Original Sin, and Salvation

B ecause the *Qur'an* does not teach the doctrine of original sin, the Islamic view of sin is not alarming. To counteract a rather casual understanding of sin, the Christian must teach what Jesus said about sin in the Sermon on the Mount. Jesus taught that breaking the spirit of the Law is just as serious, if not more so, than violating the letter of the Law. God has written His law in nature, and in the hearts of men, which individuals have to suppress in order to be able to live with their own conscience.

Because Islam does not view sin as a radical problem, it is not surprising that salvation is not viewed as a radical issue. The Muslim believes that salvation is based on good works which will, in the Day of Judgment, be weighted in a scale of balances, which can be tipped for reward, or judgment.

> "And those whose scales are heavy [with good deeds]—it is they who are the successful. But those whose scales are light—those are the ones who have lost their souls, [being] in Hell, abiding eternally" (Surah 23:102–103).

The Muslim that believes in Allah, has done many good deeds, and lived a life of righteousness, can hope to obtain salvation. In Islam, man is not a fallen creature in need of salvation, but is a noble being, a vice-regent of Allah. Man is a perfect creature, perfectly endowed to fulfill the Divine will, while being enhanced with revelation. Because he was created in the image of God, man is a perfect, innocent, and moral master of creation. Man is to fulfill the will of Allah in space and time. Man is not an object of salvation, but a subject. The Islamic religion is confident that man is morally, and essentially good, and that he is competent to obey God and fulfill the will of God.

Despite this high view of self, Islam does not offer any assurance of salvation, only an eternal hope based upon one's own self-esteem, and a self-evaluation of one's life. Many Muslims who have converted to Christ, have done so because of the assurance of salvation the Christian faith offers to all those who believe in Jesus as personal Savior.

Islam believes that Christianity emasculates men, by making individuals weak creatures that are helpless, hopeless, and in need of a Savior. Islam tells individuals they are not helpless, they are not hopeless, they can stand on their own, and take personal responsibility.

Islam is in harmony with much of the thinking of modern day philosophers such as Friedrich Nietzsche (1844–1900), who taught that the "soft underbelly" of Western society was a direct result of the elevation of Christian virtues such as grace and mercy, as opposed to strength and courage. Christianity is for the weak.

It is good to ask the Muslim who believes in Paradise and Hell, what are they being saved from, since they are basically good people. A Muslim might respond that they do believe in being saved, or rescued, from Hell. An honest Muslim, who is informed about the *Qur'an*, might even say that it is Allah who determines the destiny of an individual. Allah will determine the destiny of a person based on the weighing on a scale of justice, and their good works.

Now, because there is a scale of justice, in Islam, there must be a standard to go by. In Islam, what is required to meet this standard is a declaration of faith in Allah, and his prophet Muhammed, obligatory prayer, compulsory giving, fasting in the month of Ramadan, and making a pilgrimage to Mecca.

However, the practical problem is this. "What person could ever survive the perfect judgment of a perfect God, no matter how good they have tried to be?" The Psalmist asked, "If You, LORD, should mark iniquities, O Lord, who could stand?" (Psa. 130:3).

Herein is the problem with the Islamic view of salvation. A Muslim can never know until the Day of Judgment if the scales of judgment will tip in their favor. The Christian doctrine is that the scales of justice will never tip in favor of a person's own righteousness. Like Nebuchadnezzar, every person is weighed in the balances and found wanting (Dan. 5:27). Every person who is saved must be clothed in the righteousness of another, even Jesus Christ the Lord. The work of Christ at Calvary must be imputed, or charged to a person's account, so that in the Day of Judgment the sinner can be declared righteous in the sight of the Law of God. It is "not by works of righteousness which we have done, but according to His mercy He saved us, through the washing of regeneration and renewing of the Holy Spirit" (Titus 3:5).

To the Muslim, the Christian cries out, "Do not believe in your own essential goodness. There is no one who is good in the sight of God, for all have sinned, and sin has built a barrier between man and God. Christ has died to tear down that barrier between man and God, which is why His work of redemption must be embraced as your own. Believe on the Lord Jesus Christ and you shall be saved. Only then can you have any hope and confidence of eternal life. Eternal life is a gift of God, not something that is earned, and therefore merited. Flee from the false hope of salvation based on the five pillars of Islam, and rest on the one sure foundation, Jesus Christ and His righteousness. The just shall live by faith, not by merit."

Ironically, the *Qur'an* has passages which teach how grateful men are, how easily led astray they can be, and how often they transgress, and do bad things. So, there is a conflicting message in *Qur'an* between the rhetoric and the reality, and between various Surah passages. Islamic theologians simply ignore the intrinsic contradictions. The same tension is found in Christianity, whereby many theologians ignore the seriousness of sin.

Both Christians and Muslim must relearn some basic truths about sin. Sin, in the sight of God, is not merely doing the "big" sins of murder, lying, cheating, stealing, and blasphemy. Sin, in the sight of God, is the transgression of the Law.

Once the Law is broken, in any form, no matter how minor a person might think the transgression, then the perfection which God demands of men is gone, and can never be recovered. To live a life of virtue after a transgression is only what duty requires, it cannot cover, or heal, any past transgression.

It is this deep, and mature understanding of the nature of sin, which is not comprehended by Muslims, or many Christians. As a result, individuals feel smug, and self-righteous, because they have stopped doing something which is wrong, or they have worked extra hard to be better. It is all to no avail. "What can wash away my sin? Nothing but the blood of Jesus."

Only when a person is in Christ, can the Great Commandment be complied with. What is the Great Commandment? "You shall love the LORD your God with all your heart, with all your soul, and with all your strength" (Deut. 6:5).

No one can ever love God with all their heart, which is why sin is so serious, and which is why a Savior is needed. Every sinful soul needs someone to rescue the soul from the penalty of sin, which is Hell. Self cannot rescue self by good works. It is impossible. The standard cannot be reduced to a level of personal achievement. God is perfect, and demands that men be perfect. This divine mandate can only be achieved by the righteousness of Christ being charged to the account to those who are the heirs of salvation.

Only in Christ can a person find forgiveness of sin, with assurance that the blood of Jesus Christ will cleans from all sin, past, present, and future. Christians are commanded to make our election and salvation sure. This can only be done by embracing the promise of God in Christ.

If, in the providence of God, a Muslim comes across this writing, or if this material can be shared with a Muslim, let the word go forth, "God receiveth sinful men, even me, with all my sin." Come to Christ, because you take sin seriously.

TEN

Islam and the Scriptures

The Muslim viewpoint is this. Allah—because of man's propensity to be led astray from the path of virtue—has sent Prophets with divine revelations. Some of these Prophets, such as Moses, and Jesus, were given books, reflected in the Pentateuch, and the Gospels. Unfortunately, these books, these historical documents have been corrupted. The only true, and pure book to be trusted, was given by Allah to the last Prophet, Muhammed. All other books are no longer reliable, and therefore they are no longer authentic and authoritative. Within this frame work, with its obvious limitations, the Muslim proceeds to discuss Christianity, and the Scriptures. The dilemma, for the Muslim, is that while the theologians of the *Qur'an* teach one thing to Muslims, the *Qur'an* itself contains a different message. Within the *Qur'an* are various verses which exalt the Prophets, command people to listen to the message of the Prophets, including Jesus, and to honor the "Scriptures," meaning, the Bible.

The Gospels are to be honored.

"And let the People of the Gospel judge by what Allah has revealed therein. And whoever does not judge by what Allah has revealed—then it is those who are the defiantly disobedient" (Surah 5:47).

The Old Testament is to be honored.

"And We have revealed to you, [O Muhammad], the Book in truth, confirming that which preceded it of the Scripture and as a criterion over it. So judge between them by what Allah has revealed and do not follow their inclinations away from what has come to you of the truth. To each of you, We prescribed a law and a method. Had Allah willed, He would have made you one nation [united in religion], but [He intended] to test you in what He has given you; so race to [all that is] good. To Allah is your return all together, and He will [then] inform you concerning that over which you used to differ" (Surah 5:48).

The Bible is honored above the Qur'an,
because the Bible preceded it.

"So if you are in doubt, [O Muhammad], about that which We have revealed to you, then ask those who have been reading the Scripture before you. The truth has certainly come to you from your Lord, so never be among the doubters" (Surah 10:94).

Muslims are not to debate with Christians,
but are to believe the Bible.

"And do not argue with the People of the Scripture except in a way that is best, except for those who commit injustice among them, and say, 'We believe in that which has been revealed to us and revealed to you. And our God and your God is one; and we are Muslims [in submission] to Him'" (Surah 29:46).

Initially, Muhammed wanted to say to Jews and Christians, "I am a monotheist, I believe in the Bible, and I am a prophet like Moses and Jesus." Because Muhammed wanted his words to be taken seriously, he said what he did about the Bible. However, as time passed, as devout Muslims wanted the *Qur'an* to be authoritative, the realization came, there was a problem. The Qur'an teaches that it cannot be changed, the *Qur'an* says that Moses, and Jesus are to be honored, the *Qur'an* says that the Bible is to be trusted, and yet there are all the contradictions.

To reconcile their dilemma, later Muslims came up with *Tahrif*, or, the doctrine of corruption. *Tahrif* is an Arabic term used by Muslims for the alterations, which Islamic tradition claims Jews and Christians have made to the revealed books, specifically those that make up the *Tawrat* (or Torah), *Zabur* (possibly Psalms) and *Injil* (or Gospel).Arab scholars assert that Jews and Christians have changed the word of God.

The teaching of *Tahrif*, or the doctrine of corruption of the Bible was first taught in the tenth century, or four hundred years after Muhammed died. Ibn Hazm rejected all claims of Mosaic authorship and insisted that Ezra was the author of the Torah. He also organized arguments against the New Testament. To make the basic assertion sound modern, and scholarly, Amin Ahsan Islahi (1904–1997) wrote about four types of *Tahrif.*

One form of *Tahrif,* is to deliberately interpret something in a manner that is totally opposite to the intention of the author. To distort the pronunciation of a word, to such an extent that the word changes completely.

Another form of *Tahrif* is to add to, or delete a sentence or discourse in a manner that completely distorts the original meaning. For example, according to Islam, the Jews altered the incident of the migration of the Prophet Abraham in a manner that no one could prove that Abraham had any relationship with the *Kaaba.*

A third type of *Tahrif* is to translate a word that has two meanings, in the meaning that is totally against the context. For example, the Aramaic word used for Jesus that is equivalent to the Arabic: "ibn" was translated as "son," whereas it also meant "servant," and "slave."

Finally, to raise questions about something that is absolutely clear, in order to create uncertainty about it, or to change it completely, is *Tahrif.*[1]

That Arab scholars can unite with apostate Christian scholars to question the text of the Bible, does not resolve the problem. If the validity of the claim is bogus, so is the conclusion.

If a person is serious about finding out if the Hebrew and Greek texts of the Bible are reliable, an honest inquiry can be

---

[1] See also https://en.wikipedia.org/wiki/Tahrif.

made. One way to validate the authenticity of the Bible is to consider the prophecies that were made years, and even centuries, before they transpired. Daniel the prophet foresaw the fall of the Babylonian empire, and the rise of the Medes-Persians, the Greeks, and the Romans. It was an amazing display of foretelling the future. Isaiah prophesied about the birth, life, and death of the Messiah, Jesus.

Jesus, as a true prophet, predicted the fall of Jerusalem forty years before it happened. Jesus predicted events that no one thought was remotely possible, but it happened. In contrast, Muhammed (*c.* A.D. 570–June 8, 632), came along five hundred years later, and, allegedly, dismissed what had been prophesied. Normally, a prophet spoke of things being true, that will yet come to pass. Muhammed's position is rather unique, and silly. He, as an alleged Prophet, invalidated things that had already taken place. He said that what had taken place, and could be historically verified, never happened. That is an audacious position to take, and very irrational. What Muslim scholars did, beginning in the tenth century, was to assert a biased approach to history, in order to discredit the Bible, much like Liberal Theologians in Germany tried to do in the 19th century, in the form of Higher Criticism. Nevertheless, the attacks on the Bible continue to fail. They always have, they always will, because the word of the Lord endures forever (1 Pet. 1:25).

> "Last eve I paused beside the blacksmith's door,
>   And heard the anvil ring the vesper chime;

"Then looking in, I saw upon the floor,
    Old hammers, worn with beating years of time.

'How many anvils have you had,' said I,
    'To wear and batter all these hammers so?'
'Just one,' said he, and then with twinkling eye,
    'The anvil wears the hammers out, you know.'

And so, I thought, the Anvil of God's Word
    For ages skeptic blows have beat upon;
Yet, though the noise of falling blows was heard,
    The Anvil is unharmed, the hammers gone."[2]

If a Muslim is not willing to consider the Bible in its historical setting, because the *Qur'an* tells a person to, then all is lost, and any rational discussion is over. The only recourse a Christian has is to commend such a person to God. It is possible such a person has been given over to destruction, according to prophecy. Jesus spoke of those, "'Seeing they may see and not perceive, and hearing they may hear and not understand; lest they should turn, and *their* sins be forgiven them." (Mark 4:12)

---

[2] Attributed to John Clifford.

Disassociation and the Religious Lie of Islam

"It is the absolute right of the State to supervise the formation of public opinion." —Joseph Goebbels

"If you tell a lie big enough, and keep repeating it, people will eventually come to believe it. The lie can be maintained only for such time as the State can shield the people from the political, economic, and-or military consequences of the lie. It thus becomes vitally important for the State to use all of its powers to repress dissent, for the truth is the mortal enemy of the lie, and thus by extension, the truth is the greatest enemy of the State." —Joseph Goebbels

"And you shall know the truth, and the truth shall make you free." —Jesus Christ

"Lie not one to another . . ." —Apostle Paul

During the reign of the Nazis in Germany from 1933 to 1945, millions of people were lured to their death by the propaganda of disassociation. Simply put, the Nazis lied about what they were doing. People were peacefully lured into trucks that took them to death camps. Each step of the way the Nazis told people they were being relocated for their own good. A better tomorrow was just ahead. Like sheep led to the slaughter, millions of Germans meekly submitted to self-butchery.

Because the world has not learned this lesson from history, genocide is taking place against Christians, and other minority groups in the Middle East. This time the butchers do what they do in the name of the religion of Islam. The lie which is being told, and the disassociation which is taking place, is that all the mayhem and madness, all the murder and slaughtering of the innocent, and unsuspecting, has nothing to do with Islam. "Islam is a peaceful religion," the world is told. "Islam is being radicalized," we are told. "Islam does not seek ethnic cleansing and world domination." It simply wants to practice its own faith. Meanwhile, there is endless *jihad*.

Those who are committing the violence, do so in the name of Allah and Islam. Those who read the *Qur'an* understand what the text teaches. At least 109 verses call Muslims to war with non-believers for the sake of the rule of Islam. Some verses are very graphic. Even the simplest of mind can understand what is being said.

> "And kill them wherever you find them, and turn them out from where they have turned you out. And Al-Fitnah [disbelief or unrest] is worse than killing . . . but if they desist, then lo! Allah is forgiving and merciful. And fight them until there is no more Fitnah [disbelief and worshipping of others along with Allah] and worship is

for Allah alone. But if they cease, let there be no transgression except against Az-Zalimun (the polytheists, and wrong-doers, etc.)" (Surah 2:191–193, The Noble Qur'an).

The preceding verse to this passage (2:190) refers to "fighting for the cause of Allah those who fight you" leading some to believe that the entire passage refers to a defensive war in which Muslims are defending their homes and families. The historical context of this passage is not defensive warfare, however, since Muhammad and his Muslims had just relocated to Medina, and were not under attack by their Meccan adversaries. In fact, the verses urge offensive warfare, in that Muslims are to drive Meccans out of their own city, which they later did.[1]

Those who do not join the fight are called hypocrites, which explains, in part, why so-called peaceful Muslim do not protest the violence and bloodshedding of their fellow compatriots. Even the nominal Muslim understands that Allah will send them to Hell if they do not join the slaughter, and so millions are silent. They stay in different societies without assimilating. Millions of Muslim stay in various societies to simply wait for the moment when they can tear up the Constitution of their host nation, and embrace Sharia law. Pretending to be peaceful, pretending to "love" their new host country, they engage in commerce, and business.

They work in stores, and factories. They repair computers. But they also defend the defenseless when a conversation is engaged. They defend Islam, and the *Qur'an*. They defend the violence, and

---

[1] See www.thereligonofpeace.com.

bloodshed. They do not denounce the despicable acts their religion fosters worldwide. They do not speak up for the Jews. They do move to support, or defend the genocide of Christians in the Middle East.

Some try to make a case for moral equivalency, and insist that Islam teaches nothing different than the Old Testament verses of violence. However, unlike the Old Testament verses, the *Qur'an* leaves their passages open ended, meaning they are not bound, or restrained by historical context. The *Qur'an* presents verses of violence that guide a world by the unchanging word of Allah. These verses allow for suicide bombers in the modern world. These soulless martyrs seek salvation by offering to Allah a blood sacrifice, that of themselves, and their victims.

Time after time, weak and foolish national leaders, unite with clueless individuals to tell us that Islam has nothing to do with the obvious violence. The leaders of Islam in Iran and elsewhere, are more honest. They plainly state they will destroy the nation of Israel. They plainly demonstrate their hatred of Christians, and others, by acts of genocide. They glory in their shameful religion of Islam. They laugh at how easy it is to infiltrate nations, recruit the young, and create chaos at will.

The intellectuals, such as those at the Islamic university in Cairo, do not condemn the horrific carnage in the name of Allah. Why? Because one Muslim cannot accuse another Muslim of being a *kafir*, or infidel, as long as that person believes in Allah, and the Last Day. Muslims are taught not to condemn another Muslim, even if they commit every atrocity imaginable.

As a result of non-condemnation by Islamic intellectuals, and nominal Muslims, bombs are exploded in airports, and subways. Christians are beheaded, and their murders are posted on You Tube. Nations are terrorized, and the world, in its foolishness, accepts the language that what it is witnessing has nothing to do with the Islamic religion. It is a lie of such portion that has not been embraced since Joseph Goebbels took over the propaganda arm of the Nazi regime.

When will this madness end? It will end, when the truth is spoken. It will end when the ethics of the Christian faith are embraced. It will end, when Jesus comes to rule and reign in the hearts of individuals. It will end, when people begin to love life, and their children, more than they hate others. It will end, when we stop lying to one another. It will end when the lie of Islam is rejected. Islam cannot consistently be called a peaceful religion when there is so much teaching that permits the contrary. It is a bloody, and violent religion that seeks world domination. It denies freedom of religion, freedom of speech, freedom of worship.

Islam enslaves by the sword, and demands submission to Allah. Since Allah is not present, Muslim warriors demand submission to their religious leaders. The Christian says no to the lie of Islam, no to Sharia Law, and no to bowing to any caliph, let alone the god called Allah, a god of men's imagination. Christians bow to no one but the Lord Jesus Christ, to whom every knee shall one day bow, and call Him Lord. He alone is King of kings, and Lord of lords. *Soli Deo Gloria.*

TWELVE

Islam and Moral Equivalence

Sometime in late February, 2015, a SWAT team surrounded a home in Port St. Lucie, Florida, where some Christians were known to live. A towering man from a government agency, dressed in black body armor, placed a megaphone to his lips and spoke with a Middle Eastern accent, "I am a government agent. Come out with your hands up. You are under arrest. You are completely surrounded. You cannot escape!"

There was a long pause. A sniper, looking through his high power lens, saw a slight movement inside the house. He took aim as a woman cautiously pulled back a handful of window curtain to see something that amazed and horrified her. The Christian woman saw that she was surrounded. There were blue lights outside her home and a large van waiting to take her away. Overhead she could hear the whirl of a helicopter ready to track her movements if she dared flee. Armed men were out to arrest her. High power weapons were aimed at every window and door. Then, the voice on the megaphone sounded again.

"This is your final warning. Come out with your hands up. You have been found guilty of association with known people on the government watchlist. We has a warrant for your arrest based on events dated November 27, 1095 in connection with Pope Urban II.

Keep your hands in the air. Do not wield a gun, a knife, or a sword. Come out the front door and move down the sidewalk slowly. Do it now!"

The Christian lady inside the house, with her three children, could not believe her ears. She was being accused of participating in an event that happened nearly a millennia ago! What in the world was going on? Who would have authorized this arrest?

Then, the Christian lady had a chilling thought. The President of the United States had sanctioned this. The Christian lady remembered the news report. She had recently watched a prayer breakfast, which the President had attended, where he made some incredible remarks. On February 5, 2015, the President of the United States dared to imply there was a moral equivalence between Christians and the Islamic-murdering terrorist. It is the Muslim community that continues to behead people, drown infidels, rape women, and bash open the heads of babies by swinging their little bodies so that they hit the side of a building.

She recalled what the President said.

"Humanity has been grappling with these questions throughout human history," he told the group, speaking of the tension between the compassionate and murderous acts religion can inspire. "And lest we get on our high horse and think this is unique to some other place, remember that during the Crusades and the Inquisition, people committed terrible deeds in the name of Christ. In our home country, slavery and Jim Crow all too often was justified in the name of Christ."[1]

The message was cheered by Muslims, and embraced by atheistic, agnostics, Liberals, and a compliant news media. "Christians are morally no better than blood thirsty Muslims who kill in the name of their god, Allah."

Even though Christians today are not beheading their enemies, nor killing homosexuals, nor wielding knives, or setting off bombs to destroy or inflict pain and suffering on unsuspecting men, women, and children, there is still a moral equivalent because, after all, Christians do read a book called the Bible.

What does it matter that the Bible tells about Jesus who instructed His followers to love their enemies, and to do good to those who hurt them? All that does not matter. Christians are evil. Christians are suspects. Christians are to be rounded up and either silenced, imprisoned, or slaughtered in every form possible.

Having been born to a Muslim father, attended a madrasa in Indonesia, and raised, at least, to sympathize with the Muslim religion, the former President of the United States who make those remarks has consistently refused to call any member of ISIS a "radical Muslim terrorist," and has provided the nation of Iran with more than one hundred and fifty billion dollars to create a nuclear bomb, with additional resources to spread the Muslim faith throughout the world. Through his attitude, actions, and public comments, the former President of the United States has

---

[1] "Remarks by the President at National Prayer Breakfast." https://Obamawhitehouse.archives.gov/the-press-office/2015/02/05/remarks-president-national-prayer-breakfast (accessed, July 4, 2017).

drawn a moral equivalent between modern day Christians, and Muslims, by appealing to historical events.

Returning now the narrative. The leading government agent in the black armored gear saw the front door opened. A frightened lady emerged, followed by three children. Each had their hands in the air. All were terrified, and uncertain as to what was happening, or why.

The government agent once again picked up his megaphone to instruct several other agents under his command.

"Agent Muhammed, Agent Reed, Agent Matthews: go inside and confiscate every Bible you can find. Do it now! Go!"

The command was obeyed without question or delay.

Later, after the Christian lady was arrested, and taken to a federal prison for her "hate crimes," her children placed in protective care, and a defense lawyer was called, the events of the day were reported only on the local news. There was hearty public outcry, but the government's action was vigorously defended by the major news media outlets.

What the final outcome of this event will be is yet to be determined. What is certain, is that there is a war on the church in general, and Christians in particular. There is an effort to minimize the atrocities being committed by one religion, by making a moral equivalence with the other, based on events that took place, and ended a long time ago. It is illogical to make this comparison, it is immorally reprehensible, and it is a distortion of reality. Such is the evil that men do, even those in the highest office of the land.

Lest anyone be confused with this story, let me be clear in order to set the record straight. While the narrative of the Christian mother and her children being surrounded by U. S. federal agents in February, 2015 is fictitious, the words of the former President of the United States and the actions of numerous devout Islamic Muslims are true. Christians are being killed in the name of a bloodthirsty god, named, Allah. The *Qur'an* is being used by many as a pretext for murder, rape, robbery, torture, and terrorism. Those who embrace the Islamic religion have much to be ashamed of, because the majority of Muslims have not, and will not, denounce their fellow Muslims who deliberately hurt others.

As Christians throughout the world celebrate traditional holidays and continue their daily lives in service to God, churches are on a high state of alert against Islamic butchers who are mad with hatred in the name of their god, Allah. In contrast, the Prince of Peace, Jesus, invites every Muslim to lay their weapons against Him, and embrace Him as Lord and Savior.

When the soldiers of the Jewish High Priest struck Jesus, He said, "If I said something wrong," testify as to what is wrong. But if I spoke the truth, why did you strike me?" (John 18:23). If Jesus has done something to harm a Muslim, if a twenty-first century Christian has done something to hurt a Muslim, where is the evidence? Muslim, "Why do you hate Jesus and Christians?" Again, I ask, "Why?"

On this day, repent. Come to the One who loves sinners. He will still forgive you and save you, now. Go down on your knees and call Christ, Lord.

THIRTEEN

Decapitation and Islam: When Will the Madness Stop?

On July 26, 2016 an elderly French priest, 84 years of age, was beheaded in a hostage situation in a church south of Rouen, Normandy, in northern France. His killers were justly shot dead by French police. True to form, the American President went before a national audience and, once again, told people not to rush to judgment about Islam and reminded the world how Islam is a peaceful religion and even went so far as to suggest it may take consider time in order to fully understand the motives of such terrorists. Rational people, however, know better. We know the motive of the two terrorists, because one of the bloody Islamic religious butchers spoke from his heart. The world wonders, "When will the madness stop?"

The madness of Islamic extremism will stop when the evil it promotes is confronted, condemned, and exterminated by people of righteousness. A righteous person, is a person who has a moral compass. A righteous person, is a person who knows the Word of God, and the God of the Word, and will live out the ethics of what has been revealed. God has said, "Thou shalt not murder."

Yet, the religion of Islam gives shelter for violence and murder. The *Qur'an* contains more than 100 verses that call Muslims to war with nonbelievers (infidels, Jews and Christians) for the sake of the rule of Islam. Muslims that do not join the good fight, the *jihad*, are called hypocrites, and warned that Allah, the bloodthirsty god of this religion, will send them to Hell if they do not engage in the slaughter. "As to those who reject faith, I will punish them with terrible agony in this world and in the Hereafter, nor will they have anyone to help" (Surah 3:56).

The *Qur'an* does not have any context to end violence other than universal capitulation to an Islamic caliphate. Therefore, year after year, generation after generation, individuals read the *Qur'an*, embrace the violent ideology, and go out to spill blood, preferably on the holy altar of a Christian church.

The madness of Islamic extremism will end when the leaders of civilized nations realize that they are not safe, and neither are their citizens. Most national leaders live in a protected environment of luxury. They have food, and clothing, and personal security. They do not risk having their heads cut off, or their bodies slashed with machetes. They are not afraid of bombs going off. But they should be, because the Islamic barbarians are coming after the leaders of every nation, just as quickly as they can.

The madness of Islamic extremism will end when the religion of Islam fades into the dustbin of history. There are nobler religions to embrace. I commend the Judeo-Christian religion to every thoughtful Muslim who feels unsafe, and is sick of their bloodthirsty religion. Leave the hatred, hostility, bloodshed, and violence behind. Judaism offers the Moral Law of God to live by.

Christianity offers redemption, forgiveness, grace, and the hope of heaven, which is by faith in the Lord Jesus Christ. Let the word go forth in the Muslim community, there is a better way to live. Repent. Convert. Come to Christ. Save yourselves.

The madness of Islamic extremism will end when Muslims begin to love their children and their families more than they hate Jews and Christians. Young Muslim men and women invite death because the Muslim religion is a cult of death. Young people embrace death even if they have a wife or children. How tragic it is for children to be born into and indoctrinated into a cult of death. It is good for them. "Fighting is prescribed for you, and ye dislike it. But it is possible that ye dislike a thing which is good for you, and that ye love a thing which is bad for you. But Allah knoweth, and ye know not" (Surah 2:216).

The madness of Islamic extremism will end when the martial legacy of Muhammad ceases to be glorified. His real legacy is a trail of blood and tears, in the sands of Arabia, and on the streets of numerous nations. The real legacy of Muhammad is that of children being run over by a bus, hacked body parts on the streets of Brussels, Germany, and France, and the head of a Catholic priest laid on an altar. When mass murderers, such as those found in ISIS, are glorified by their religious leaders, and are not universally condemned by the followers of Islam as having no plausible interpretation of the religious texts, then the religion of Islam remains without dignity, or moral direction.

Jesus Christ is the Prince of Peace who is truly worthy of honor and glory. His precepts are precious. His promises are true. His counsel to love is wise. There is life, not death in the One who came to give life, and that more abundantly, to all who follow Him.

Many Muslims have bravely come to Christ. They have replaced the *Qur'an* with the Bible. They have put away their hatred for their Jewish brethren, according to the flesh, as children of Abraham. They have renounced violence. They have sought God's forgiveness for refusing to love others. That is good. Every person who moves away from Islam, moves towards ending the evil extremism of that religion. *Sola Deo Gloria*.

FOURTEEN

The Violence of Islam and Christianity

Perhaps one reason why much of professing Christendom's condemnation of the violence of Islam is not as effective as it could be is due to a principle Jesus spoke of in Matthew 7.

> "Judge not, that you be not judged. ²For with what judgment you judge, you will be judged; and with the measure you use, it will be measured back to you. ³And why do you look at the speck in your brother's eye, but do not consider the plank in your own eye? ⁴Or how can you say to your brother, 'Let me remove the speck from your eye'; and look, a plank *is* in your own eye? ⁵Hypocrite! First remove the plank from your own eye, and then you will see clearly to remove the speck from your brother's eye" (Matt. 7:1–5).

The truth of the matter is there is a lot of violence within churches too. True, the violence is primarily verbal in American churches (and I'm sure the same holds true throughout the rest of the world), with attempts to hurt ministers and ministries economically mixed with slanderous conversations, and libelous writings. Nevertheless, the hatred in the heart is real. Jesus declared that in the sight of God this hatred in the heart is soul murder, and is worthy of judgment. "But I say to you that whoever is angry with his brother without a cause shall be in danger of the judgment. And whoever says to his brother, 'Raca!' shall be in danger of the council. But whoever says, 'You fool!' shall be in danger of hell fire" (Matt. 5:22).

Lest anyone doubt there is much violence in Christendom, then I invite individuals to simply attend a monthly congregational meeting or official board meeting of the local church. Soon after the meeting is called to order the verbal violence will begin, along with parliamentary maneuvering to get their way. Angry words are spoken. Next comes the questioning of motives, the assigning of motives, and finally there is an open assault on a person's character, and spiritual labors. Driving all of this verbal violence, is the will to power.

I do not say that *every* church meeting (or even most) is characterized by verbal violence and secret agendas. I do say such meetings happen far too often and undermines an effective Christian life and witness. There is a better way, and that is to do God's work God's way. Undergirding doing God's work God's way is a willingness to submit to the principles and practices that guided the New Testament churches.

First, there should be a desire to cooperate, and not compete with one another. The Bible calls this "preferring one another." "*Be* kindly affectionate to one another with brotherly love, in honor giving preference to one another" (Rom. 12:10).

Second, there should be a willingness to give honor and respect to the Word of God and not force upon the assembly any secular human document, or parliamentary book. The church should be a church of one book only, the Bible. When chapter and verse can be cited for a practice, then argumentation should end, and implementation of the known will of the Lord should begin. The Lord promised to guide His people and give them peace, provided they listen to Him.

> "But the Helper, the Holy Spirit, whom the Father will send in My name, He will teach you all things, and bring to your remembrance all things that I said to you. [27] Peace I leave with you, My peace I give to you; not as the world gives do I give to you. Let not your heart be troubled, neither let it be afraid" (John 14:26–27).

Third, there must be humility, not the desire for pre-eminence. "*Let* nothing *be done* through selfish ambition or conceit, but in lowliness of mind let each esteem others better than himself. [4] Let each of you look out not only for his own interests, but also for the interests of others" (Phil. 2:3–4).

The main difference between the violence within Christendom, and the violence within the Muslim community, is not a contrast between love and hate. Rather, the contrast is between official state support of violence, which much of Islam enjoys, and governmental restraint placed upon the violence that individuals in the church would do to one another if they could. Until there is an addressing of this undercurrent of violence within the hearts of individuals that influence the congregations of

American churches, there is not much hope for a spiritual impact on the Muslim culture.

FIFTEEN

Islam and the Face of Evil

Within the Muslim community there is a particularly barbaric practice. That is to say, throughout the world, millions of young girls have been subjected to the painful rite of passage that involves cutting off their genitals. It is estimated that some 3,000,000 girls each year are at risk for 1 of 4 types of female genital mutilation (FGM).[1] Even within the boundaries of the United States, thousands of girls are subject to the brutal ordeal of female genital mutilation. Since 1990, the amount of FGM has tripled.[2] Not surprisingly, the number has exploded among immigrants from predominantly Islamic countries. In order to curb the sexual desire of girls and preserve their sexual honor prior to marriage, Muslim parents allow the clitoris of girls to be cut. Many of the girls bleed to death or die of infection. Those who

---

[1] FGM can be classified into four categories: clitoridectomy, the partial or total removal of the clitoris; excision, partial or total removal of the clitoris and the labia minora; infibulation, narrowing of the vaginal opening by sewing together folds of skins; and, other harmful procedures such as pricking, piercing, cauterizing, scraping, and incising. See also, Krupa, Michelle. "The Alarming Rise of Female Genital Mutilation in America." CNN.com http://www.cnn.com2017/05/11/health/female-genital-mutilation-fgm-explainer-trnd/ (accessed July 8, 2017).

[2] Ibid.

survive often suffer severe health issues during marriage and pregnancy (not to mention the emotional trauma inherent in such a practice). Though twenty six states in America allow this barbaric practice, there is a federal Law against the practice. On April 14, 2017, a Michigan emergency room doctor was arrested and charged with performing female genital mutilation on many girls about the age of seven.[3]

"Female genital mutilation constitutes a particularly brutal form of violence against women and girls. It is also a serious federal felony in the United States," Daniel Lemisch, acting U.S. attorney for the Eastern District of Michigan, said in a statement. "The practice has no place in modern society and those who perform FGM on minors will be held accountable under federal law."

Christianity, by contrast, does not allow for any brutal, and inhuman treatment of women.[4] Christ came to honor and esteems all women. Jesus invites women, from every nation, to be a follower of His, in order to be treated with dignity and respect. "There is neither Jew nor Greek, there is neither slave nor free, there is neither male nor female; for you are all one in Christ Jesus" (Gal. 3:28).

---

[3] See also, Baldas, Tresa. "Feds Drop Bombshell: Up to 100 girls may have had their genitals cut in Michigan." Freep.com. http://www.freep.com/story/news/2017/06/07/female-genital-mutilation-doctors-michigan/378219001/(accessed July 8, 2017).

[4] Despite what you might read in the above cited CNN article, FGM is not practiced among Christian communities. CNN never provides any examples or factual data to back up this claim. More likely, the news story carelessly includes Christianity as a religion that practices FGM so as not to give the (correct) impression the practice is chiefly supported by and practiced among practitioners of the religion of Islam.

Christian men are to nurture, and protect their wives, and to love them as Christ loved the Church, meaning men are to love their wives in a sacrificial manner. "Husbands, love your wives, just as Christ also loved the church and gave Himself for her" (Eph. 5:25).

Muslim women will find mercy from God, love from Christ, and protection in the Church. Respect, esteem, and honor is offered to women because of Christ. Jesus never hurt any woman, nor does He allow His followers to mutilate them.

As Muslims have enslaved and mutilated women, even up to this present hour, so the Muslims have enslaved men, women, and children in the African community. History records that Muslim Arabs hunted, enslaved, tortured and killed over 140 million ethnic Africans for more than a thousand years. While Christians in Western Europe are not innocent of the barbaric slave trade, civilized nations have stopped the inhumane practice. In contrast, human slavery by Arabs continues today in the Middle East. While Jesus came to make men free, Muhammad bought, kept, and sold, African slaves. Documentation of the African Arab slave trade is documented by John Allembillah Azumah in his important book, *The Legacy of Arab-Islam in Africa.*

Again, it is worth repeating: the fruit of such a religion speaks volumes.

SIXTEEN

The Twelfth Imam

A unique characteristic of the Muslim world is its ability to thrive on chaos. No matter what historical contribution Muslims have contributed to society—and some of the contributions are, indeed, significant—there is a self-destructive facet of the society reflected in the expectation of the Twelfth Imam, or Mahdi.

The coming of the Twelfth Imam, a belief held by 85 percent of those identifying as Shiite Muslims, will mark a catastrophic period in world history. Shiite Muslims believe that a series of Imams were appointed to carry on the message of the Prophet, Muhammad. These special Imams rank above all other prophets, except for Muhammad himself. The Twelfth Imam, Muhammad al-Mahdi, is believed to have been born in Iraq in A.D. 869, and never to have died. He is in hiding and will one day re-emerge as a messiah, with Jesus, to bring peace to the world and establish Islam as the ruling faith in every country on the globe.

The Twelfth Imam, the Mahdi, will make himself known when the world is in the throes of total chaos and war. What is of concern to many world leaders is the idea held by some Shiite

Muslims that the emergence of the Twelfth Imam can be forced by starting an apocalyptic conflict. Former Iranian president Mahmoud Ahmadinejad believes that Muslims can hasten the coming of the Mahdi by starting a nuclear confrontation simply by instigating a cataclysmic strike, perhaps by attacking Israel, with that nation's inevitable retaliation. Certainly, the Twelfth Imam would then appear.

The seriousness of Ahmadinejad is reflected in the fact that he has called for the reappearance of the Twelfth Imam from the podium of the United Nations General Assembly in New York City. Is it any wonder that the Bible commands God's people to pray for the peace of Jerusalem? "Pray for the peace of Jerusalem: may they prosper who love you" (Psa. 122:6).

When NBC News' Ann Curry interviewed Ahmadinejad in Tehran in September 2009, she asked him about the Mahdi:

> "CURRY: In your speeches, you pray for God to hasten the arrival of the hidden Imam, the Muslim messiah. Would you tell us, as I know you will speak about this at the general assembly, as well. What is your relationship with the hidden Imam, and how soon do you think before the second coming?
>
> AHMADINEJAD: Yes, that's true. I prayed for the arrival of the 12th Imam. The owner of the age, as we call him. Because the owner of the age is the symbol of the— justice and brotherly love prevailing around the world. When the Imam arrives, all of these problems will be resolved. And a prayer for the owner of the age is nothing

but a wish for justice and brotherly love to prevail around the world. And it's an obligation a person takes upon himself to always think about brotherly love. And also to treating others as equals. All people can establish such a connection with the Imam of the age. It's roughly the same as the relationship which exists between Christians and the Christ.

They speak with Jesus Christ and they are sure that Christ hears them. And responds. Therefore, this is not limited to us only. Any person can talk with the Imam.

CURRY: You've said that you believe that his arrival, the apocalypse, would happen in your own lifetime. What do you believe that you should do to hasten his arrival?

AHMADINEJAD: I have never said such a thing.

CURRY: Ah, forgive me.

AHMADINEJAD: I—I—I was talking about peace.

CURRY: Forgive me.

AHMADINEJAD: What is being said about an apocalyptic war and—global war, things of that nature. This is what the Zionists are claiming. Imam . . . will come with logic, with culture, with science. He will come so that there is no more war. No more enmity, hatred. No more conflict. He will call on everyone to enter a brotherly love. Of course, he will return with Jesus Christ. The two will come back together. And working together, they would fill this world with love. The stories that have been disseminated around the world about extensive war, apocalyptic wars, so on and so forth, these are false."[1]

If history teaches anything, it teaches that when the face of evil speaks, people should listen. Individuals mean what they say. People will tell you exactly what they plan to do, and so must be taken seriously. Adolf Hitler spoke of invading Russia in his book, *Mein Kampf*. The world did not listen. Barack Hussain Obama said he would destroy the coal mine industry if elected president and support the slaughter of the unborn through the barbaric organization called Planned Parent. Millions did not take him seriously and elected him twice to be President of the United States. As a result, many miners were put out of work, and the slaughter of the innocent continued. Shiite Muslims tell the world plainly of their belief the Twelfth Imam and of their desire to have him emerge. The world must take the violent religion of Islam seriously. Al Qaeda, ISIS, which considers itself the "Islamic Caliphate," or a theological empire, Hamas, and Boko Haram, are speaking with one loud and violent voice.

The fanaticism of Islam is found in their jihads. In 2017, in a genocidal frenzy, ninety-thousand Christians were slaughtered in the Middle East in the name of Allah. In Paris, Germany, Russia, and America, devout Muslims slaughter men, women, and

---

[1] Source, Bridget Johnson, June 21, 2014, ThoughtCo.

children indiscriminately. The scourge of the Islamic faith must be wiped from the face of the earth. There is no other alternative apart from the grace of God converting Muslims in mass to Jesus Christ.

Every Christian can pray to that end. But every nation should be prepared to defend itself from the nuclear holocaust to come, if Muslim rulers have their way in the world.

SEVENTEEN

The Inherent Evil

O n May 23, 2017, ISIS stepped forth to claim responsibility for a cowardly attack in Manchester England which left at least 22 people dead and more than 59 people injured after a suicide bomber tagged an Ariana Grande concert.

Just hours before United States President Trump had been speaking in Saudi Arabia drawing a distinction between radical Islamic terrorist and the religion of Islam, as if the two can be separated. They cannot.

As long as the religion of Islam exists, devout followers of the blood-thirsty god they call Allah, and its foundational butcher, Muhammad, will understand what the prophet taught, and will want to be obedient to this false god and barbaric prophet. The religion of Islam is not a religion of peace but submission or death in a violent way. Even those who do submit to Islam are not safe, or free, as Muslim women well know, and as Sharia law dictates.

The message of Islam, reflected in the *Qur'an*, and espoused by its clerics, is plain enough for a child to understand. "*La ilaha illa Allah*," meaning, "None has the right to be worshipped except Allah."

In practice, what this religious mantra means is that freedom of religion is not an Islamic virtue. No devout Muslim can possibly honor or respect a document such as the Bill of Rights which is part of the Constitution of the United States. This truth has practical implication in American for millions of devout Muslims who live in the United States. They live here under false pretenses. They live here to undermine Christian values. They live here—if they are to be consistent with their foundational beliefs—to one day to rise up and strike, just as the suicide bomber infiltrated London and lived there until the hour came for him to rise up and kill as many infidels as possible.

Why? Because infidels have no right to the pursuit of life, liberty, and happiness. Why? Because infidels do not worship the god Allah, a god that demands violent and untimely death on the unsuspecting, including women, young people, and children. Why? Because no one has the right to be worshipped except Allah.

Adding insult to injury, the majority of Muslim leaders throughout the world refuse to openly denounce the atrocities committed in the name of Allah and Islam. They either passively, or actively, support the actions of their more devout Muslims brothers and sisters of the faith. Then, Muslims have the audacity to pretend that the *Qur'an* does not teach the slaughter of the infidel, as if rational and educated people cannot read.

Clever Muslims teach their followers how to answer what the "lying eyes" of the world can plainly see, the slaughter of the innocent. Some Muslims speak with smooth words to deceive the innocent and keep good people from rising up in horror to protest

Islam. These silver tongued wordsmiths try to convince non-Muslims that they, and their religion, is simply misunderstood.

Muslim charlatans argue that the main word for "kill; slay; or slaughter" is not *jihad*, it is *qital* and refers to combat.

Question. "With whom are Muslims to engage in combat with?"

Answer. "Muslims are to engage in combat with those who oppose the Islamic religion. Muslims are to stand up for righteousness and strive to prevent oppression, aggression, and tyranny."

With this sort of circular reasoning the religion of Islam will forever spill blood in the sand of the Middle East, blow up stadiums, and denote bombs wherever infidels are gathered, terrorize anyone, and everyone who disagrees with them and does not submit to the god Allah, and has absolutely no respect for the prophet Muhammad.

If evil is defined as injurious behavior to self and to others, then, indeed, Islam is an evil religion. The evidence is there for the world to see. But, there are none so blind as those who refuse to look.

Because the religion of Islam must be driven from civilized societies and off the face of the earth, how is it to be defeated? The answer is the power of the gospel, and the person and work of the Lord Jesus Christ.

The Gospel offers individuals love and life. The Gospel brings peace to hearts and minds. The Gospel tells people to do good to others, and to do them no harm. The Gospel is the power of God unto salvation. It blasts the rock-like resistance of the sin-hardened heart. The rough jailor in Philippi, the runaway slave Onesimus in Rome, and Saul the persecutor on the Damascus road, all had the hard core of their resistance broken by the Gospel. They were changed by the power of the Gospel and their lives were transformed forever. One day the Gospel will penetrate the Muslim world to defeat the tyranny of evil produced by the *Qur'an*.

Then, there is Christ. The book of Hebrews reveals the superiority of Christ. "But we see Jesus, who was made a little lower than the angels, for the suffering of death crowned with glory and honor, that He, by the grace of God, might taste death for everyone" (Heb. 2:9). God has crowned Christ with glory and honor because He is worthy for He gave His life a ransom for the many. While Mohammad and his devout followers take lives, Jesus gave His life as atonement for sin. One day every knee shall bow and every tongue shall confess that Jesus Christ is Lord. *Sola Deo Gloria.* To God be the glory!

EIGHTEEN

Believe the Gospel

"Now after John was put in prison, Jesus came to Galilee, preaching the gospel of the kingdom of God, [15] and saying, 'The time is fulfilled, and the kingdom of God is at hand. Repent, and believe in the gospel'" (Mark 1:14–15).

When word reached the ears of the people of Palestine that John the Baptist had been arrested, there was shock and dismay.

"What happened?"

"How could this be?"

"What did he do?"

And the story was told in a simple sentence: John would not keep silent in the presence of public sin. The private behavior of Herod the Tetrarch (Luke 3:19) and Herodias had become the public scandal and shame of the nation. Herod had taken his brother's wife for himself.

But it was not marital infidelity alone that John preached against. John rebuked the ruler of the land "for all the evils which Herod had done" (Luke 3:19). From the ministry of John three principles are established.

First, there is right and there is wrong in life regardless of what people with power, prestige, or personal wealth say, or do. God has written His Law in stone, summarized in the Ten Commandments, and God has written righteousness on the consciousness of every soul that comes to any level of maturity. John rebuked Herod because this is a moral universe and nothing will ever change that.

Second, there cannot be a separation of church and state, or religion and politics, because the attitude and actions of government officials affect the moral fabric of society by which families are held together. Religion is not a component of life; religion is life.

Religious beliefs permeate every facet of human existence and affects how we eat, drink, sleep, work, talk and dress. This truth is reflected by the way the Pauline epistles are written. They are written in two parts, doctrinal and practice. The first three chapters of Ephesians, are doctrinal while the last three chapters are practical. Someone has said that all doctrine should be practical, and all practice should be doctrinal.

Third, there is Moral Evil in the world. John rebuked the ruler "for all the evils which Herod had done." The "evil" John has in view here is *moral* evil. The moral evil that men do must be distinguished from *natural* evil. There are harmful things that come to us in life, but not because of personal wrongdoing. Rather, some evil comes because of the presence of sin in the universe itself. In Luke 13 there are two illustrations of this concept.

First, the story is told of some citizens in Galilee who were murdered without mercy by Pilate. Then Jesus mentioned a tower in the town of Siloam which collapsed. Eighteen people were killed. These Natural Evils of political murder, and accidental deaths, did not happen because of any Moral Evil on the part of those individuals who were hurt, but because of the presence of sin in the universe.

This distinction between Moral Evil, for which an individual will be judged, and Natural Evil, which an individual cannot control, is important because there are tragic events in life.

A parent who has a child that is afflicted with a physical ailment, or a person who has contract a deadly disease might be tempted to believe themselves to be great sinners. Like the man born blind in John 9 the heart wonders, "Lord, who has sinned that such a thing should happen?" There is great guilt. But, it is a false guilt. There is comfort in the teaching of Jesus who explained that sometimes Natural Evil is allowed in order to manifest the glory of God. It is God Himself who has allowed this. Exodus 4:11 explains. "So the LORD said to him, "Who has made man's mouth? Or who makes the mute, the deaf, the seeing, or the blind? *Have* not I, the LORD?"

God does not hesitate to take responsibility for all that happens in the Universe of His creation, and by so responds to that which might be called "surd evil." The word "surd" is from the Latin *surdus* and means to be "deaf," "silent," "stupid." When applied to God, one of two charges is often made. It is sometimes argued that God is certainly powerful, but since He does not prevent evil, He must not be altogether good. Others have argued God is certainly good, but since He does not prevent evil, He must not be altogether powerful.

Some years ago a Jewish rabbi had a son with a rare disease by which the child aged rapidly. Not too many years had passed before the child looked like an old man. And then, the child died. Reflecting upon the ordeal, the Rabbi wrote a book to address the question, *Why Do Bad Things Happen To Good People?* The author's conclusion was that that bad things happen to good people because God means well, but He is not able to control His universe. This is an example of surd Evil, and it is wrong.

God is always sovereign and He has done something about the essence of evil. God has sent Jesus Christ into the world to deal with every form of evil so that we read that after "John was put in prison, Jesus came into Galilee" (Mark 1:14).

Bodily and boldly the Son of the Living God visited a particular geographical location, and our hearts cry out to heaven, "Come to us, Lord! Come to us!" In the form of the gospel Jesus does come to individuals today. Those who have ears to hear can listen afresh to His message. "The time is fulfilled, and the Kingdom of God is at hand; repent, and believe the gospel."

Notice the fourfold message of the Messiah beginning with the statement that "the time is fulfilled." In context the Lord Jesus was referring to the fulfillment of the prophecy given to Daniel.

While he was in exile in the land of Babylon, Daniel was presented with a calendar of coming events. It was revealed to the prophet of God that in 483 years Messiah would appear. The prophetic clock started to tick when a king by the name of Artaxerxes issued a decree in 457 B.C. allowing the Jews to return to their homeland. Jerusalem was going to be restored and rebuilt. Then, according to prophecy, 483 years later, Messiah, Jesus, the Anointed One was baptized and began His public ministry. And in this we learn a spiritual truth.

God always keeps His word and He keeps it on time. God has never yet said anything that did not come to pass in the appointed hour and so we read the words of Galatians 4. "But when the fullness of the time had come, God sent forth His Son, born of a woman, born under the law, to redeem those who were under the law, that we might receive the adoption as sons." (Gal. 4:4–5).

The second part of the Message of the Messiah is that the kingdom of God is at hand. The phrase, "Kingdom of God," is used often in Scripture. What this phrase means is that rule of God, the divine kingly authority has been entrusted to the Person of Jesus Christ (Luke 22:29). The Kingdom and the King of the Kingdom has come into history. Because the Kingdom of God has come to earth in a very real way, there are several facts that can be noted about this unique kingdom. For example, the Kingdom of God is designed to save. The purpose of the Divine rule is to redeem men from the power and pollution of sin (1 Cor. 15:23–28).

Second, the Kingdom of God stands opposed to the "Kingdom of this Word" (Rev. 1:5), which is under the authority of Satan (Matt. 4:8; Luke 4:5). The opposition between the Kingdom of God and the Kingdom of this World is real and intense. A spiritual battle will rage until the destruction of Satan Himself (2 Cor. 4:4).

Third, the Kingdom of God is supernatural. It cannot be explained by gimmicks and gadgets, budgets and buildings, promotions and pressure. One of the largest movements in the country today is the Church Growth Institute. Unfortunately, so much of what is suggested for building the local assembly is natural. In fact, it is fleshly. The Kingdom of God cannot be explained by the devices and designs of men.

- Only God can defeat Satan.
- Only God can destroy death (1 Cor. 15:26).
- Only God can raise the dead to incorruptible bodies (1 Cor. 15:50).
- Only God can make a soul stop wanting to sin.
- Only God can restore the earth to Paradise (Matt. 19:28).
- Only God can change the hardened heart of a man or woman clever enough to live a religiously hypocritical life as Nicodemus.

Then fourth, the Kingdom of God cannot be destroyed. It can be rejected (Matt. 23:13), and it can be opposed—by Communism, Atheism, and every other religion in the world, but it cannot be destroyed.

Because of the permanency of the Kingdom of God perhaps it would be wise for individuals to repent and come under the rule and reign of the Sovereign of the Kingdom of God, even Jesus Christ the Lord. That is the third point of the message of the Messiah.

Now, for repentance to happen, there must a measure of genuine sorrow for sin. This is a fundamental problem because sorrow for sin is no longer natural to the heart, since the Fall. Sin hardens the heart.

Karl Menninger realized the hardness of the human heart and wrote a book, published in 1975, *Whatever Became of Sin?* As a psychiatrist Dr. Menninger saw patient after patient with mental illness, and only one thing in common, they had no sorrow for what they had done in life, no matter how much pain and sorrow their attitudes and actions caused.

The Bible is right. The heart is desperately wicked, and deceitful. People pretend to be one thing in public and act very differently in private. If there is to be any gospel repentance, there must be sorrow for wrong actions, meaning the evil that has been done. If there is to be any true sorrow, then God must grant repentance as a gift of grace, and He will, to those who ask for it. We can say this with great confidence because the very word "gospel" contains this concept.

The English word "gospel" comes from the Anglo-Saxon "god spell," or "God's story."

The Gospel is God's story of the way of eternal salvation, and that way is through Jesus Christ the Lord.

For time and for eternity it is good news that God has sent Christ to deliver us from the burden, the power, pollution, and presence of sin which is why Christians love to testify to faith in Christ and exhort others to believe the gospel.

"Would you be free from the burden of sin?

There's power in the blood,
    Power in the blood;

Would you over evil a victory win?
    There's wonderful power in the blood.

Would you be free from your passion and pride?
    There's power in the blood;
Power in the blood;

Come for a cleansing to Calvary's tide;
    There's wonderful power in the blood."

Believe the gospel—that, simply stated, is the message of the Messiah.

Appendix

The Qur'an: A Critical Book Review

BY ADAM MURRELL

CONSIDERED without question by Muslims to be the infallible and inerrant word of God, the *Qur'an* is the holy and sacred revelations given to Muhammad by the prophet Gabriel in the early seventh century. Originally transmitted in the Arabic language, the *Qur'an* provides Muslims with the duties required of them, as well as basic rules for living. Except in a few places where an angel or prophet is speaking, the majority of the text is the words of Allah himself. For the Western reader who might be cognizant of some basic rules of grammar, the style of speaking might seem peculiar. That is to say, when reading through the *Qur'an*, one might notice the unorthodox use of tenses when God is speaking. Sometimes he starts in the third person and then changes to the first person in the same sentence (7:180–184). Another aspect that makes for less-than-helpful reading is the form in which the writings have been collected and transmitted to us today. Arranged in order of length over against chronology, deciphering the progressive revelation Muhammad received is not always easy and might seem to stand at open variance with previous statements—if one does not understand the current context in which the statements were given.

One can easily become frustrated and disenchanted, at many points, with the seeming tension between two irreconcilable positions. For instance, the student of the book, perhaps, wants to know: Does the *Qur'an* teach its followers to inflict harm upon non-believers? Some point to Surah 9:5 which would seem to indicate it is the obligation of every Muslim to "slay the idolaters wherever you find them." However, the *Qur'an* also teaches that God does not love aggressors (2:190). So which verse takes precedence and why? The same conflict resolution needs to be implemented in a host of other doctrines including the role and inherent worth of men versus women. Indeed, it seems that there are ample passages pertaining to a number of controversial doctrines that cannot be harmonized apart from spiritualizing or allegorizing the text, in which case, any number of beliefs can be concocted to fit the current day's thinking.

Nevertheless, among the centrality of all doctrines enumerated in the holy book is a strong monotheistic message that emphasizes Allah's forgiveness and mercy towards those who display absolute submission to his will. That said, the one who reads the *Qur'an*, either as a religious adherent or as a dispassionate observer, would perhaps most want to reflect upon three important doctrines that are significant in the quest to understanding important aspects of Islamic thought, namely, God, salvation, and the afterlife.

According to the *Qur'an*, Allah's unity, the *tawhid*, is stated in both positive and negative terms. That is to say, the holy book teaches unequivocally as to what Allah is and is not. For instance, the *Qur'an* speaks that "Allah is One" (112:1). He is a singular unity that is comprised of only one person sharing one being over against the aberrant Christian view of the Godhead. To Muslims, the Christian perspective of God is blasphemous and amounts to *shirk*, idol worship. The *Qur'an* goes to great lengths to repudiate the God of Christianity and makes clear references to the religion when it states, "He begot none, nor was He begotten. None is equal to Him" (112:1–4). The reference is clearly a denial of God begetting Christ or the latter being begotten by the former (cf. Psa. 2:7; John 1:18, 3:16; 2 Cor. 5:21; 1 John 4:9; etc.). Allah is not three, but one. Indeed, the Trinity is clearly antithetical to the monotheistic concept of Allah as revealed in the *Qur'an*. "Unbelievers are those who that say: 'Allah is one of three.' There is but one God" (5:73).

Jesus Christ, therefore, is not to be equated with Allah as the Christians do. "Unbelievers are those who declare: 'Allah is the Messiah, the son of Mary'" (5:17; 72). Moreover, Jesus is said to be "no more than an apostle" (5:75). The unbeliever, namely, Christians, who continue to equate Jesus with God and refuse to repent, will be "cast into the fire of Hell" (5:73–74). Just as Yahweh was serious about placing anyone or anything before or beside Him, the *Qur'an* forbids the same practice. While adherents of both religions claim monotheism, Yahweh, as revealed in the New Testament, has manifested Himself as three persons sharing one being (Trinitarianism), while the *Qur'an* teaches Unitarianism. Any other view, as the *Qur'an* stresses, abrogates the clarity of the holy book and amounts to polytheism.

In attempting to help believers understand Allah more fully, the *Qur'an* reveals some of the attributes or qualities of God. It speaks highly of his mercy and forgiveness (4:110; 6:12; 8:38), though severely of those who fail to submit wholeheartedly to him both in this life and the one to come (8:38–39; 41:28, 40–42). Furthermore, Allah, similar to the God of the Jews and Christians, sees all things (40:20), is omnipresent (2:115; 7:7), possesses omniscience (2:268; 10:61), is omnipotent (6:61–62; 5:19), and created the universe and all its inhabitants (2:29; 3:191; 6:1; 46:33). Without question, Allah manifests all of these attributes and many more. He is not limited by anyone or anything. In fact, he is eternal; he is infinite (112:1). It would seem, therefore, that the Muslim could rightly proclaim as Matthew did that with God all things are possible (Matt. 19:26).

Allah is also love but not in the same sense as Yahweh is love. In Islam, the greatest act of love Allah accomplished is that he forgives some of their sins. More than this, he also provides sustenance for his creation, gives families and friends, shows mercy to the believing, and gave humanity his divine revelation in the *Qur'an*. It could also be said that an aspect of his love is persistence in that Allah does not immediately destroy unbelievers but grants them repeated opportunities to repent of their wrongdoing and unfaithfulness and submit wholly to him.

That Allah is good and righteous means the faithful follower can spend eternity with him in Paradise provided he has fulfilled all the conditions necessary for eternal life. Salvation is granted to all who perform good deeds. "Blessed is the reward of those who do good works" (3:134–139). However, good works are not enough to gain entrance into paradise. Faith must be present and active alongside of deeds. Indeed, Allah promises believers who exercise faith and perform good works will have an eternal reward (5:9).

This is not to say, however, that one can earn the forgiveness of Allah. In fact, one must rely upon Allah's grace and mercy in order to achieve forgiveness and salvation in paradise. The reward of everlasting life with him is based upon his grace. "Allah chooses whom He will for His mercy. His grace is infinite" (2:105; cf. 8:29).

For the wrongdoer, however, his fate is far worse. The one who refuses to submit himself to Allah, believe in him, and fails to perform good deeds, will face unimaginable suffering on the Day of Judgment when his fate will be sealed. Allah prepared a fire for him wherein he will scream out for water in agony, only to receive scolding water and persist in a place where there is no rest (18:30; cf. 3:131; 19:59–61).

Since one's ultimate destiny will determine whether he goes to heaven or hell, the followers of Islam attempt to placate Allah through their own efforts. This is necessary since there is no intercessor who pleads on the behalf of another, as the Christians with the intermediary, Christ. Therefore, one must continue to be obedient toward Allah, obey his commands as expressed in the Qur'an, exercise faith, and repent sincerely so that he may be forgiven (3:16).

Those who fail to do all these commands, after having been justly warned by the revelation of the Qur'an and the prophets, will deservedly be punished for his obstinacy (3:77). In hell, the impenitent and unfaithful will face eternal torment, suffering that will "assail them from every side, yet they shall not die" (14:17). Whether the pictures described in the *Qur'an* are literal or metaphorical and much like the Christian view of hell, the reality is that the suffering endured there is unimaginable and far worse than even the human mind can comprehend.

As painful as hell is, however, heaven is the antithesis of perdition. Paradise is a blissful state in a "lofty garden," replete with fruit to enjoy, to eat and drink to one's content (69:21–24). Moreover, and perhaps more importantly, believers who enter into paradise—for those who had faith and did good works—will be "wedded to chaste virgins" (4:57). That one receives these promised blessings, therefore, is incumbent upon his continual faith, obedience, and submission to Allah and his word and be accompanied with a sincere repentance of sins. If he does that, he does not have to worry about suffering through an eternity of hell but will receive the loving-kindness of Allah's mercy and grace (3:135; 7:8–9; 49:14). And if one thinks he will live his life in a self-serving manner, only to repent at his final breath, he is sorely mistaken. For with Allah, he is not to be deceived. "Allah is wise and all-knowing. But Allah will not forgive those who do evil all their lives and, when death comes to them, say: 'Now we repent!'" (4:18).

When working through the *Qur'an*, one cannot help but to reach the conclusion that Judaism and Christianity played an integral role in shaping the thoughts of Muhammad and can be seen through many parallels in his teaching and thinking. That said, however, it is also evident that Islam defines itself in response to the latter and is Muhammad's attempt at rehabilitating the teachings of which he was aware. The student of Christianity might easily come to the conclusion the prophet Muhammad was confused on a number of Christian teachings and attempted to amalgamate a hybrid between Judeo-Christian beliefs and what he believed to be true concerning the nature of God and what would prove most beneficial to him and the advancement of his own personal agenda.

Reading through the *Qur'an*, therefore, was truly an exercise in patience in seeing an attempt made to improve upon the doctrine of God, man, sin, salvation—among many others—but failing miserably on the most fundamental level. That which is *theopneustos*, God-breathed (2 Tim. 3:16), cannot be improved upon as the *Qur'an* so amply demonstrates.

www.ingramcontent.com/pod-product-compliance
Lightning Source LLC
Chambersburg PA
CBHW060304050426
42448CB00009B/1746